FIELD ARCHAEOLOGIST'S SURVIVAL GUIDE

FIELD ARCHAEOLOGIST'S
SURVIVAL GUIDE

Getting a Job and
Working in
Cultural Resource
Management

By
CHRIS WEBSTER

Left
Coast
Press
inc.

WALNUT CREEK, CALIFORNIA

LEFT COAST PRESS, INC.
1630 North Main Street, #400
Walnut Creek, CA 94596
http://www.LCoastPress.com

ISBN 978-1-61132-928-5 paperback
ISBN 978-1-61132-930-8 consumer eBook

Library of Congress Cataloging-in-Publication Data

Webster, Chris, 1975-
  Field archaeologist's survival guide : getting a job and working in cultural resource
management / by Chris Webster.
     pages cm
  Includes bibliographical references and index.
  ISBN 978-1-61132-928-5 (pbk. : alk. paper)—ISBN 978-1-61132-930-8 (consumer ebook)
  1. Archaeology—Vocational guidance. 2. Archaeology—Fieldwork. 3. Cultural property—Protection. 4. Antiquities—Collection and preservation. I. Title.
  CC107.W43 2014
  930.1--dc23
                            2014002535

Printed in the United States of America

∞ ™ The paper used in this publication meets the minimum requirements of American
National Standard for Information Sciences—Permanence of Paper for Printed Library
Materials, ANSI/NISO Z39.48–1992.

green press INITIATIVE

Left Coast Press, Inc. is committed to preserving ancient
forests and natural resources. We elected to print this title on
30% post consumer recycled paper, processed chlorine free. As
a result, for this printing, we have saved:

1 Trees (40' tall and 6-8" diameter)
1 Million BTUs of Total Energy
111 Pounds of Greenhouse Gases
606 Gallons of Wastewater
41 Pounds of Solid Waste

Left Coast Press, Inc. made this paper choice because our
printer, Thomson-Shore, Inc., is a member of Green Press
Initiative, a nonprofit program dedicated to supporting
authors, publishers, and suppliers in their efforts to reduce
their use of fiber obtained from endangered forests.

For more information, visit www.greenpressinitiative.org

Environmental impact estimates were made using the Environmental Defense
Paper Calculator. For more information visit: www.papercalculator.org.

To the underappreciated thousands of field technicians
that never get the respect they deserve,
this is for you. Thank you.

CONTENTS

LIST OF TABLES

PREFACE

Cultural resource management (CRM) archaeology is a fun and rewarding job if you want it to be. We choose when and where we want to work. If we want to move to a different city, state, or region, we pick up and go. Want to excavate pueblos in the southwest? Go for it. Want to do long surveys in the high desert of Nevada? No problem. We are masters of our own destinies. We take vacations when we want to, and powerful people with high-paying jobs want to be us. Why, then, do people leave this field? Why are most of the field technicians you meet in their twenties?

The problem is that field technicians are never taught how to live on the road. They come out of college filled with idealized visions of what it is like to be an archaeologist, and when they get to their first project, the shocking reality sets in. After a 10-day session of eating gas station breakfast burritos and other fast food, most people are ready to pack it in. We stay, though, because we love this job. We love being archaeologists, and many of us won't let anything stand in the way of our goals.

This book is designed to give everyone that travels and lives on the road for a living a few ideas on how to improve their quality of life. Aside from airline pilots and traveling salespeople, I don't know of any other non-military profession where you spend so much time away from home. In fact, many archaeologists don't even have a true home to go back to. So, we live on the road, and we do our jobs.

Most of us aren't taught how to write a résumé or curriculum vitae, how to write a cover letter, or what to say in an interview. We aren't told about important websites like Shovelbums.org and archaeologyfieldwork.com. No one shows us how to use a compass, sketch out a map, or even what Universal Transverse Mercator coordinates are. We aren't told how to get the best deals on hotels, how to make those hotels livable for many days at a time, or how to make healthy, nutritious meals on the road. This book will help with all of those things and more.

I am by no means an expert on all things related to shovelbumming or living on the road. What I am is a field archaeologist that has traveled around the country, worked many different jobs, and lived in countless hotel rooms. I've meet a number of amazing people in my career, and I've learned a lot from them. There have also been many mistakes along the way. I'm sure I've lost a great deal of money, time, and a certain amount of sanity by trying to figure some of this out on my own. Most of us are reluctant to ask questions because we don't want to seem like we don't know what we're doing. I'm no different. That's why this book is in your hands right now though. You are asking the questions, and I'm providing some of the answers.

Acknowledgements

This book would have been impossible if it weren't for the help of the many field technicians and crew chiefs I've worked with along the way. I learned from a lot of people and incorporated what they did and how they did it into my own style. One person from whom I learned a lot about companies and getting jobs is Shawn Olson. I met Shawn on my very first project, and we've been friends ever since. He was even in my wedding. For my first few years in archaeology, I always called Shawn before applying to a new company. He'd been in the business for a long time and knew just about everyone. Shawn would tell me what he knew about the company and whether I should work there or not. His advice was, and is, invaluable. Our metaphysical and science-based conversations were a welcome addition to most days in the field too.

The number of people I've learned archaeology skills from is immeasurable. There have been so many people in so many different states that I can't keep track. I always try to take some bit of knowledge that I didn't have before from every project I've been on. My first major excavation was in downtown Miami, and it included a lot of great archaeologists. The Well Crew, as we were known, were a great bunch of people, and I owe a lot to them. You know who you are. The friends I've made in archaeology have all contributed in different ways to the attitude I have developed and the way I think about the profession and the people in it. The conversations I've had on philosophical and scientific topics have been great. Some of the best conversations were had with (even though we didn't always agree on things) Blake Cochran, Deanna Dytchkowskyj, David Field, Shannon Iverson, Richard McDaniel, Shawn Olson, and too many others to list.

During the final stages of this book I asked for any tips and advice that others in the field would like to give to new shovelbums. I received some great comments from a number of people and included them in this book. Those people are Russell Alleen-Willems, Jeffrey Baker, Wilbur Barrick, Jim Christensen, John Dougherty, Justin Dunnavant, David Field, Jennifer McGuire, Brandon McIntosh, Jamie Palmer, Andrew Sewell, and Bill White.

One person that deserves my thanks, and more than I can give, is my wife, Rachel Roden. I met Rachel on my very first project, and we started dating about a year later. From then on, we traveled the country and worked on every project together until she left the field in 2011 to pursue another passion. Rachel always stuck with me through the good times and the bad. She was there when my passion got me fired and when my forcefulness created awkward situations with our supervisors. She stuck by me and encouraged me to keep going when I started my company, and I had no income for the better part of a year. Without Rachel's support, this book would not have been possible.

Finally, I need to thank Brian Fagan and the publishers at Left Coast Press. After reading Fagan's *Writing Archaeology: Telling Stories about the Past*, I was encouraged to put my thoughts down on paper and write this book. I showed a very early draft to Caryn Berg and Mitch Allen at Left Coast Press during the 2013 Society for American Archaeology Annual Meeting in Hawaii, and they encouraged me to submit a proposal. Apparently they liked it! Caryn's advice and editorial expertise made the book great, and it wouldn't be what it is without her.

Any errors or opinions in this book are entirely my own. If you disagree with anything I've said, then I encourage you to publish your own opinions! We need more people to speak out about this field so others can learn from our mistakes. Start a blog, produce a podcast, or write a book. Do whatever you can to bring archaeology and the real life of an archaeologist to light. When the project report is turned in, your job is only half done. The other half is communication and education. Tell people what you do and how you do it. Be proud of your job, your passion, and your work regardless of the level you are at.

INTRODUCTION

I'm sitting in the student lounge of Babcock Hall at the University of North Dakota in Grand Forks (UND). I'm essentially on vacation from the construction job I took after graduating in the spring, and I'm waiting for my upcoming trip to Africa to dig in Olduvai Gorge with the Earthwatch Foundation. A friend that graduated the year before me walks in, and we chat about why he's there. Hurricane Katrina had just destroyed his apartment and the offices of the business he worked for in New Orleans. When the conversation turned to what we were going to do next, he asked if I'd checked the archaeology job position website at www.shovelbums.org (Shovelbums) yet. The rest of my life would be affected by that question.

The story above took place in autumn, 2005. When my friend mentioned the website, Shovelbums, I was shocked that I hadn't heard of it. Also, I was embarrassed that I didn't really know what cultural resource management (CRM) archaeology was. He was patient with me and told me to check the website for jobs, and that as long as I had a field school and a degree, I would be able to look for short-term archaeology jobs across the country. I had no idea.

I remember learning about CRM in my introduction to anthropology class about five years before that; however, it was just a bullet point on a slide and was never discussed again. The Earthwatch Expedition I was about to go on would count as a field school, and of course, I had recently earned my degree in anthropology, so I started looking on the Shovelbums website.

I applied for a few jobs, but since I had no experience, I wasn't surprised when no one called me before I left for Africa. After returning from the field school, I remained in North Dakota. I kept applying for jobs, but the "no experience" part was killing my chances of anything. Luckily, I'd taken a class called "senior seminar" during my last semester at UND and had learned how to write a *curriculum vitae* (CV) and a cover letter. I retooled my CV to reflect leadership experience and classroom experience that I thought would be relevant to CRM. I was particularly proud of the osteology class I took and the sketches of every bone in the human body that I drew. I was sure to highlight that. I sent out the new CV to a few more companies and kept looking for work in the area. Fortunately, a few friends from college were working on a dig with a CRM company just over the river in East Grand Forks, Minnesota. I called the project manager and she agreed to let me work there. I finally had my first paying archaeology job! My work wasn't done, though. Not by a long shot.

During my first few weeks on the job, I learned what Universal Transverse Mercator (UTM) coordinates were, how to dig a 5-cm level in a 2-m square unit 2–3 m below the surface, how to identify fire-cracked rock (FCR), how to use a standing shaker screen, and how to water screen. Every activity I did on that site was a new experience for me. Let me say that again: every activity I did on that site was a new experience for me. That's one reason I decided to write this book.

Some people learn in field school how to survey, how to use a compass, how to dig and record an excavation unit, and a number of other common tasks. Some people don't. The problem lies with a disconnect between knowing what you want to do for a career and choosing the right field school to make that happen. It seems like many people choose a field school based on either what country they want to go visit or on what their school has to offer. No one is being counseled on taking a field school that will actually teach you what you NEED to know, rather than what you WANT to know.

What we need is a single university class that teaches people about the field of CRM archaeology. Of course, you could spend an entire four years on the subject if it was done right, but you have to start somewhere. The class would ideally teach students about CRM, the laws that govern and dictate what it is and how it operates, and the ways CRM is undertaken across the country. After finishing the class, a student could choose to shovel test in the southeast and look for historic and prehistoric sites. Or, she could decide that pedestrian survey and mining sites are more interesting and decide to work in the Great Basin. The student could then apply for a field school that would at least be in that same region but would also teach them how archaeology is typically studied and recorded there. Since classes like that simply don't exist in most universities, I decided to write this book.

Organization

This book is designed to take a person from college, to the workforce, to unemployment or retirement. A typical CRM field technician will usually work in a region or across the country for a few seasons. They'll get frustrated with moving and eventually rent an apartment. After not being able to find a local archaeology job, they'll go work somewhere else just to pay the rent. After that happens, most never return to archaeology. I hope to change that by showing field technicians how they can improve their quality of life and learn to enjoy the lifestyle that CRM can provide rather than resent it for constantly keeping them away from family, friends, and stability.

The first section is all about getting an education and a job. Getting the right education is the key to your future success. Of course, the only way to do that is to understand the field you are going into and the options that you have across the country. CRM archaeology is very different in just about every state. Whether it's the laws, environment, or testing methods, there is always something new to learn if you are working in a different area. Section 1 will also show you the basics of creating a CV, a cover letter, and will even cover some interview basics. If you think you know everything about these topics, give it a read anyway. Some of the information might surprise you.

Section 2 really gets into the nuts and bolts of shovelbumming. This isn't like any other job, so you shouldn't treat it like any other job. That being said, there is a way to live in a hotel room or tent that will leave you content and happy rather than lonely and unsettled. I often find that the real reason people get out of this business is because they don't know how to live as a transient worker and be happy at the same time. This section has some great tips on how to live as a shovelbum, and it contains some of the essentials that every shovelbum should know.

Mapping is a big part of all forms of archaeology. You will never see a site that wasn't mapped in some sort of way. The third section begins with a discussion about UTM coordinates and what they are. Many people use UTMs every day and don't know where they come from or how they are generated. Other fundamentals of mapping and location are discussed as well and include the Township and Range system and the Smithsonian Trinomial system for site numbering. The section concludes with a discussion about hand drawing maps and how and why it should be done. You may start your CRM career using a high-end Global Positioning System (GPS), like a Trimble sub-meter, but you won't be an outstanding mapper until you map a site by hand and understand what environmental features and other items need to be mapped and which ones can be ignored.

The fourth section covers a few things that just didn't fit in the other sections, but that I thought you should know. As archaeologists, we are constantly learning, and there is always something new to find out and study.

The end of a CRM career for most people means either moving to a different field, or filing for unemployment, and then moving to another field. Most people do not retire. For one thing, the field is too young and many firm owners are still working after 40 years in CRM. Some of them may have saved up enough money to retire, but most probably haven't. Section 5 is all about the end of the career, whether it's after two years or 40 years.

Disclaimer

I am by no means an expert on everything that I'll discuss in this book. It's just really important to me that this information gets out to people so that everyone can be happier with their personal lives and therefore happier at work and more productive. Whenever I could, I consulted with colleagues and friends in this field from across the country and incorporated their advice into these pages. The only way we can all be truly successful is by working cooperatively and by learning from each other. Never be afraid to ask questions.

SECTION 1

GETTING A JOB

You can't start a career in cultural resource management (CRM) archaeology without jumping through a few hoops first. This isn't like some jobs where you can work your way up from the mail room to project manager. There are certain requirements for each position, and you simply won't get hired without them. There are people working today without some of these educational requirements, but they started in a time when that was possible. For the most part, that time has passed.

This section covers education, preparing a curriculum vitae (CV) or résumé, writing a cover letter, job hunting, and the interview process. There are a lot of resources on writing a CV, résumé, and cover letter, and on job hunting and interviewing. However, most of those resources are tailored for more traditional jobs and not for archaeology. The next few chapters, though, are designed to quickly and efficiently get you working in a region you want to work in. Check out William "Bill" White's excellent eBook on résumé writing called *Résumé-Writing For Archaeologists* (2013).

1 EDUCATION

I transferred to the University of North Dakota (UND) as a commercial aviation major. Having come from what was basically a tech school for pilots, the liberal arts environment at UND was liberating and daunting. I couldn't believe the number of classes that were available for me to take. Of course, I had to fulfill my general education requirements; so I filled them up with anthropology classes.

Since I was a little boy, I'd always wanted to be one of three things: an astronaut, an archaeologist (thanks, in large part, to Indiana Jones), or a pilot. Two out of three isn't bad. I took as many anthropology classes as I could while I was pursuing my aviation degree. During that time, I was always excited to go to the anthropology classes. They helped engage my brain and kept me interested. The aviation classes, on the other hand, were all about memorization. I loved flying, but I didn't know if I really wanted to do it for a living. I also didn't know how to make archaeology a career without being on television or being a professor, neither of which seemed possible for me at the time. So, I continued with aviation. Eventually, I switched to anthropology, and through a round-about way, I became a cultural resource management (CRM) archaeologist.

The Basics

In order to work in CRM, you need a Bachelor of Arts or a Bachelor of Science degree and a field school. That's it. The rest are details. Well, there are a lot of details and variations to obtaining those two requirements. Let's talk about them. First, though, why take anthropology classes at all?

Why Study Anthropology or Archaeology?

Some would say that taking an anthropology class is an "easy A"—a quick way to get your general education requirements out of the way so you can move on to "more interesting" things. The easy part is mostly true. Why is it true? Because deep down, everyone wants to be an archaeologist. It's true, not because the classes are easy, but because they are interesting and engaging.

Field Archaeologist's Survival Guide: Getting a Job and Working in Cultural Resource Management by Chris Webster pp. 18–22 ©2014 Left Coast Press, Inc. All rights reserved.

A few people will attend their first archaeology or anthropology class with the intention of becoming the next Dr. Jones, complete with a tweed jacket and an office filled with artifacts (until they realize that he's a grave robber and a criminal). A number of us, though, came to CRM in other ways. Some leisurely take classes without a clear objective in mind, and then, all of a sudden, they graduate and have no idea what to do next. Then, they find out about CRM and find their first job. Others, like myself, took archaeology and anthropology classes to fill in the general education requirements while pursuing another degree, but with a difference—I continued to take anthropology classes throughout my time in college.

The Author's Story

After four years and changing majors twice, I found that there was one remaining constant in my life: anthropology. In fact, for every semester I was in college, I attended at least one anthropology related class. Over the summer before my last year, I decided to pursue an anthropology degree and formally declared my major. I don't know whether the department head was thrilled or worried (I always asked a lot of questions and held up class, I'm sure). She was the best instructor I had though, and I'm sure she thought I was the best student ever! Anyway, I had taken so many anthropology classes already that only two semesters at 15 credits each of higher-level classes would complete my degree.

> **THE ESSENTIALS**
>
> College Degree in Anthropology, Archaeology, History or other suitable course of study
>
> Field School

After a very tough year of papers and research, I received my shinny new Bachelor of Arts degree in Anthropology. To celebrate, I went straight to work as a day laborer for a home remodeling company. My degree really came in handy while I was making trash runs to the dump. I was able to interpret the stratigraphy in the piles of garbage, and I was able to understand the culture of the various people working in that fine establishment. Can you hear the bitterness and sarcasm? Wait a minute. We were talking about how to get a job in archaeology. I hate to be the one to tell you this, but sometimes the path is long and arduous. Archaeology, in all its forms, consists of a small sect of fiercely passionate academics (whether you work for a university or not, we are all academics), and it's tough to break into this discipline. Eventually, I found out about the website Shovelbums.org in October of the following autumn, started my first job in early November, and never looked back.

What Classes to Take

The scope of this book isn't large enough to go into the various programs in archaeology and anthropology at institutions across the country. What you should focus on at your university is on what you want to do after graduation. Take the classes that will help you achieve that goal.

In my experience, most people currently in anthropology programs imagine themselves in the field with the "natives" after they graduate and eventually landing a tenured job at a university somewhere. It's probably not going to happen. There just aren't enough opportunities in that sector. There are plenty of opportunities, however, in CRM archaeology. You just have to know where to look. What I'm getting at is that you decide the reality of your situation early so you can take classes that will benefit you later. If you decide to go into the field where most of the archaeology in the United States is accomplished (ahem . . . CRM), then take classes that will help you get there. Classes in theory and lab work are a big help. The theory classes give you the ability to speak somewhat intelligently about a subject and the lab classes get you introduced to the tedious nature of keeping meticulous records.

If you plan to stay in the region that your university is located in, then you should probably take as many regional courses as you can. Most universities have archaeology classes focused on the state or region in which they are situated. If your school has any preservation law classes over at the law school, you might want to see if you can get in on some of them. A working knowledge of the laws and regulations that make our jobs possible and necessary will put you one step ahead. If one is offered by your university, a CRM class would be even better than a law class. Such a class will focus on the laws and regulations directly related to the formation and practice of CRM.

Finally, operate as much equipment as you can (Figure 1.1). Force yourself

FIGURE 1.1: The total station.

into a position where you can work the equipment. Use Global Positioning Systems (GPSs), total stations, magnetometers, and whatever else you can find. If you get to your first job and no one gives you the time of day because you're "green," that will all change when you walk up to the total station and you and the crew chief are the only ones that know how to use it.

Field School

Every job posting I've ever seen has required attendance in a field school (Figure 1.2) along with a degree. What they don't tell you is that most employers are only concerned with whether or not you went to field school, not what you learned there. Students tend to see this as a chance to either do something that will help them later in their careers, see other countries, or fulfill their dreams. I chose the last one, since I didn't know what CRM archaeology was when I graduated. I wish I'd chosen a program that would help me later in my career.

UND offered a field school that was located in the south-central part of the state. There was an ongoing excavation at a Native American site near Bismarck. Honestly, I don't remember any more about the project. I was so uninterested that I just didn't care. My focus was on paleoanthropology. I did not want to know what people were doing 200 years ago—I wanted to know how people became people. So, I found a field school that would let me do that.

My field school was actually an Earthwatch Expedition (www.earthwatch.org) to Tanzania where we excavated in Olduvai Gorge. It doesn't get more "paleoanthropological" than that. The Earthwatch trip wasn't a traditional field school. Anyone can do it; there is no education requirement. I did, however, learn a lot about excavation and managing finds in a lab; I wouldn't trade the experience for anything.

As fun as it was, the Earthwatch field school did not prepare me for CRM archaeology the way the UND field school would have. If I'd known about CRM, I would have researched what part of the country I wanted to

FIGURE 1.2: Olduvai Gorge field school

work in, and then found a university offering a field school that matched that interest. Field schools out here in the Great Basin do everything from excavation to standard pedestrian survey. I wish someone had told me to think about my choices a little more thoroughly so I could have better prepared myself for the future (e.g. learn about the total station in Figure 1.1).

The founder of Shovelbums.org, R. Joe Brandon, publishes a field school guide on the Shovelbums website every year in early spring. That gives you plenty of time to find a program and make plans to attend. You can choose to have one last fling with university archaeology, or you can prepare yourself for a life in the trenches with the real archaeologists. Choose wisely.

Summary

You have some big decisions to make. These are decisions that will carry you through your first few years in CRM archaeology. After a few seasons, you'll find out that it all levels out and that you're just like everyone else. There will always be that one person that's done everything, but they are an outlier—don't worry about them. Take classes that will help you in your career but do not forget to slip in a few fun ones. Most people only go to college once and you don't want to miss out on a fun class. Choose your field school wisely. You can go for practical or go for fantasy—sometimes you can have both. Whatever you do, don't stop learning.

There are a number of ways a person can approach a career in CRM. All of them require you to keep learning. Sometimes that means going to regional or national conferences, and sometimes it means reading the latest papers and popular books. Either way, learning is a part of being a professional archaeologist.

2 THE CURRICULUM VITAE & THE RÉSUMÉ

My wife, a former cultural resource management (CRM) archaeologist, and I were working in the lab, and our project manager called us in to ask about a few curriculum vitae (CVs) that had come in recently for an upcoming field project. He'd already discarded some of them because they looked really bad, and the formatting was disorganized. He asked us if we knew any of the people who's CVs remained. A couple looked promising, and he put them in a pile for CVs he wanted to look at later. Before even reading these applicant's qualifications, he had discarded over half of the CVs because of poor formatting and sloppy grammar.

You just finished walking across the stage at graduation, and you're ready to be an archaeologist. Now you just have to wait for that job to come to you, and your dreams of whip-cracking, Nazi-chasing fun can begin. Sadly, that's not how it works, and if you don't have a CV already, then you're a little behind the curve. Before we find out what a CV is and how to design one, lets first talk about the difference between a CV and a résumé.

What's the Difference?

First, curriculum vitae is Latin and roughly translates to "course of life." The plural is curricula vitae, or "courses of life." In the US, a CV, as used in academic circles, is a comprehensive and detailed list of educational achievements, work history, publications, and qualifications. A résumé, on the other hand, is a short—usually one page—document that highlights education and experience related to the specific job you are seeking[1]. A résumé is formatted to fit the particular job you are applying for. So, if you apply to ten different jobs in one day, it is conceivable that you could have ten differently formatted résumés. The CV, however, will only change as you gain experience and education. The CV is typically used in CRM—even if the job posting asks for a résumé. Some people use the words interchangeably, but employers are certainly looking for a detailed listing of your education and experience.

Field Archaeologist's Survival Guide: Getting a Job and Working in Cultural Resource Management by Chris Webster pp. 23–28 ©2014 Left Coast Press, Inc. All rights reserved.

> A résumé is a short document that highlights education and experience in order to get a particular job.
>
> A curriculum vitae is a long document that lists all education, job history, and qualifications that apply to a particular career.

The best way to craft your CV is to look at examples of other CVs. There is no one way that is generally accepted. The CV I've used since I entered CRM archaeology has never undergone a format change; however, the content has changed dramatically. Learning what to put in the CV, as someone with no paid archaeological experience, is the difficult task that awaits most new graduates. I was fortunate to have a class during my last semester at the University of North Dakota (UND) that was designed to prepare you for the multitude of career opportunities available to an anthropology graduate. One of our major tasks was to create a CV. Our professors asked us to create one on our own and bring it to class before they gave any instruction on formatting and content. I was upset that I had no archaeology experience to put in the document and came in with a short two page CV. I quickly learned how to market skills I didn't even know I had.

By the time the assignment was over, several weeks later, I had a seven page CV that was loaded with experience and accolades. What my professors taught me was that everyone has experiences that can benefit them on the job. Even though I had no archaeology experience—I didn't even have a field school at that point—my CV was loaded with experience I gained in the Navy and from work experience prior to, and during, college. For the last couple years of school, I was the president of the anthropology club; management of that organization was featured heavily on my CV. My skills, with computers and photography, ended up as bullet points at the end.

As I progressed through my career, my CV changed as I gained experience. Projects on which I was a crew chief replaced college leadership examples. Skills and abilities from college were replaced by bullet points that included a working knowledge of mapping, total station proficiency, and submeter global positioning system proficiency. My CV is still seven pages, but the content contains about 95 percent archaeological experience as opposed to none when I started. I've left some of my US Navy accomplishments in, as well as several other bullet points, because I feel they contribute to my personality and my leadership abilities.

When crafting your very first CV, take a step back and look at your life. Were you a shift manager at a fast food restaurant in high school? Did you complete a research project in college? Do you have any special skills? Are you a strong public speaker? Do you belong to any clubs or organizations? Have you been to any professional conferences, and better yet, have you presented papers at one or more? If you took a field school, did you learn how to use any equipment or how to excavate, survey, or process artifacts? These experiences should all be on your CV. Don't lie about your qualifications, but also don't be afraid to talk yourself up and make yourself look good. They are your experiences, and you earned them.

Content Order

When an employer puts out a call for employees, they should, and usually do, specify the minimum qualifications. That should be the first thing an employer sees on your CV. If you don't meet the minimums then why should they bother looking through the rest of the document?

Education

My CV starts with my education right at the top, just below my name and contact information. I list my master's degree first and then my bachelor's degree. I always list items on my CV in order of precedence. For "education," that means your highest degree first. Don't include high school. That's implied by the required college degree. Under each degree, I include my GPA and my major courses of study. If you don't have a high GPA then don't list it.

Summary

My CV used to continue with work experience at this point. However, recently I changed it to include a summary of experience and qualifications required for upper-level work in Nevada. I have a pie chart that breaks down my overall work experience in months (required by the Bureau of Land Management for permitting). I also have my current permitted status, any certificates I hold (e.g., Mine Safety and Health Administration Certification), and the organizations I belong to and for how long I've belonged to them (e.g., Register of Professional Archaeologists).

Membership in archaeological organizations can help you and should go on your CV. Regional and national memberships show that you are a professional and are dedicated to continuing education. Also, look to see if there are any volunteer archaeological or geological societies near you. They not only look good on a CV but can be a fun and rewarding experience as well.

Field School

If you don't have any archaeological work experience, then the first thing in your second section should be your field school. My field school is now actually listed after my work experience. With my education and amount of work experience, a field school is implied, and it's no longer necessary to list it at the top.

Work History

The third section will be your work history. Again, if you don't have any archaeological experience, then you have to be creative. Include unpaid positions like club officer and volunteer leadership positions. You don't have to receive a paycheck for something for it to be a valuable experience. There are different philosophies regarding the order of the work experience. I prefer to list the most recent jobs first, since these are likely to highlight my greatest qualifications. It's important to show potential employers that you have been recently employed, and that your last job wasn't three years ago. If you include the last job first, then they can quickly see that you've worked recently. It's all about not wasting their time. If you waste their time, your CV may end up in the trash.

If this is your first CV, don't be afraid to detail the classes you took in college and what you learned from them. I detailed my osteology class on my first CV. It included the rigorous weekly testing schedule and the book of sketches that we created throughout the semester that included at least two sides of every bone in the human body. This one set of bullet points got me my second job in archaeology—an excavation with hundreds of disarticulated Native American burials spanning at least ten millennia. That was an amazing project, and I would not have been hired based on my archaeological experience alone.

Additional Experience and Qualifications

The remaining sections will depend upon the individual. My CV lists my military education and experience on a single page following my work experience. If you were involved in a major organization where you received valuable experience, you should include it in a separate section so you can give more detail. For example, if you were in the Civil Air Patrol or the Boy/Girl Scouts for many years, that experience should be detailed.

The last section on my CV is called "Computers and Technology." In that section, I've listed computer programs and operating systems that I've worked with in the past. I've also listed current programming and application development projects that I'm involved in.

Formatting

There are many ways you can make your CV stand out among the hundreds that an employer is going to receive when they publish a job posting. The pie chart on the first page of my CV is an example. I guarantee that most employers don't normally see something like that, and it will stick out as unique. A friend of mine has worked in so many places for so long that he has a graph that shows how much time he has spent in different states. Find a way to make yourself stand out. Some employers receive hundreds of CVs for a single job posting. Don't let yours get "filed" before they get a chance to look at it.

FORMATTING RULES

Clean and simple

Easy to read

Don't let a job split across a page if you can help it

Spell check

Your CV should be clean and simple. Don't include long paragraphs of text. Trust me, no one is going to read them. Use bullets and clear, concise, sentences and phrases. Format all of your job experiences the same way. I list the company, followed by the geographic region, the dates I was employed, the lead person in charge, my position, and my responsibilities. If you can, include the official name of the project and/or the official site number.

The minutia should be clearly formatted as well. I start each major section on its own page with a large, clear, heading. Each section has a horizontal line at the end, right after the last item. It's clean and clear that this is the end of the section. The footer contains my name followed by the page number. Make sure major entries are not broken up over a page break unless it is absolutely necessary. It's OK to have a few extra blank lines at the bottom of any one page in order to start an entry at the top of the next page. My work experience is about three or four pages long and sometimes I have to add a few spaces after one job entry so the next one starts at the top of the page. It's little touches like that that employers probably won't notice. They will notice, however, if you have a cluttered CV that doesn't flow well. They are looking for mistakes and for a reason to put your pages in the trash instead of in the "call" pile. You are competing against people with years of experience; take the time to do it right, and make yourself stand out by not making any big mistakes.

Finally, don't call the file for your CV on your computer, "My CV". If you want an employer to take you seriously, then give it a professional file name. Usually you will send three PDFs to a potential employer. They include your CV, your Cover Letter, and your References. My file names correspond to those titles:

Chris Webster CV.pdf
Chris Webster Cover Letter.pdf
Chris Webster References.pdf

You may be able to include all of your documents in one PDF. It just depends upon the requirements of the person you are sending them to. If you can include them all in one file then name it something like, "Chris Webster Application Requirements.PDF." Just make sure that your name is in there so the employer doesn't have to hunt for it. Also, don't send a Word document unless they specifically ask for one. Always send a PDF; it preserves your formatting and is more professional.

Summary

HAVE SOMEONE LOOK OVER YOUR CV! It would be even better if that someone were a CRM archaeologist or a former employer. Get as much feedback as you can. Think about one thing for a moment. If your CV gets you a three month excavation job, when you factor in pay and per diem, that CV was worth about $9,000! Don't just throw it together, because it's probably one of the most important things you will ever do if you want a career in CRM.

Remember, every person in CRM had a first job. Every person, at one time, had absolutely no experience. We all started at the beginning.

Notes

1 William White, *Résumé-Writing for Archaeologists* (Tucson, AZ: Succinct Research, 2013).

3 THE COVER LETTER

*I have many cover letters in a folder on my computer. Always keep ev-
erything digital. It doesn't take up space, and you never know when you
might need it again. Many cultural resource management archaeologists
have worked for the same company multiple times, and sometimes you
have to send in your information again. If you have the original cover
letter, all you'd have to do is change the date and a few details. Being
a happy and successful CRM archaeologist is all about organization.
Being organized will also help you in your daily life.*

You might wonder why the *cover letter* chapter is after the curriculum vitae
(CV) chapter since the cover letter, as implied by its name, goes on top of
the CV and is the first thing an employer sees. Good catch! I'll tell you why.
In most cases, you won't draft a cover letter until you are applying for a
job. Each cover letter is tailored to the job for which you are applying. If
you apply for ten jobs today then you should have ten cover letters by the
time you're done. I'll explain why in a moment. So, before you apply for a
job, you should have finished your CV first. That's why the cover letter
comes next.

Types of Cover Letters[1]

Invited Cover Letter

As a CRM archaeologist, most of the cover letters you'll write will be what's
known as an *invited cover letter*. This means you are applying to a known
job opening that was posted or advertised somewhere. There are two other
types of cover letters that are used less often but that could benefit you in
your job search.

Prospecting Cover Letter

This type of cover letter could be useful at the start of the field season. Use
it when you are sending your CV out to potential employers that have not
advertised for a position. While I've never used this approach, I can certainly see its usefulness. One company I worked for didn't often advertise
for temporary positions and relied on a local network of field techs. The

only way to obtain a position with this company is to have already worked for them in the past or to know someone that works there. Personally, I would have appreciated a fresh perspective and would have looked over a random CV if it came in–especially if it had a fancy cover letter.

Networking Letter

If you know a former employer doesn't have any positions available right now, but might know someone in the same region that does, then a *networking letter* might be a good idea. Send this type of cover letter, with your CV and references, if you would like a little help in your job search. I've received phone calls that were basically *networking cover letters*. Everyone in CRM gets those calls in the spring. Usually a friend calls and asks whether you know of any work in the area. The *networking cover letter* is the more professional version of the buddy call.

Parts of a Cover Letter

Cover letters are essentially a standard business letter and have a predictable format. Stick with the format so a potential employer knows what to expect and can quickly scan your letter for a particular piece of information. A cover letter has five parts: heading, introduction, body, contact information, and closing. I'll take them in order.

The Heading

The heading includes your address in the upper right corner followed by the date the next line down on the left, a space, and the contact information for the person responsible for hiring at your future company. I always include a subject line as well. It usually says, "In reference to Shovelbums job posting," or something to that effect.

THE FIVE PARTS OF A COVER LETTER

Heading

Introduction

Body

Contact Information

Closing

The Introduction

The salutation precedes the introduction paragraph. It's OK to write, "Dear", or simply, "Mr. or Ms. (name)." If you do not know the name of the person who should receive the letter, you can use, "To Whom It May Concern" or the name of the company.

Included in the introduction paragraph is information regarding where you heard about the posting and the position for which you're applying. Employers often advertise on multiple websites and for multiple positions. Beginning with a paragraph stating where you heard about the job and what position you are applying for puts the employer in the right frame of mind to read your letter and your CV. Also, this is the first item of yours that an employer is going to read. Make sure it is professional and to the point.

The Body

The body can be one paragraph or multiple paragraphs. Keep in mind, though, that the cover letter should not exceed one side of one page. The body section is a place for you to sell yourself to your future employer and for you to highlight bullet points on your CV. For CRM, I sometimes include details about my availability followed by a brief accounting of my work experience and my leadership experience. Tailor the section for the job you are seeking. If you are looking for a job in the Southwest then highlight your Southwestern experience. However, if you don't have any experience in the Southwest, highlight experience at other jobs that could translate to the position. If you know what type of project you're applying for, try to highlight experience that would benefit that project. For example, if the project is an excavation, you could mention total station proficiency, mapping proficiency, and other excavation related tasks.

Contact Information

The final paragraph is where you put your contact information. Include phone numbers and email addresses. Also, include the times that you can be reached and your availability. If you plan to visit the employer or call them in the future, you can mention that there. Be cautious, however, about directly contacting employers. They receive many applications for jobs, and generally don't want to see you unless they plan to hire you.

Closing

Close the letter with a simple "thank you" or "sincerely." Don't get fancy. Leave about five lines of space after the closing before you type your name. That way you can include your signature between your name and the closing. You should find a way to get your signature on to your computer. Several PDF programs have the ability to help you create a signature for adding to PDFs. Whether you are emailing the document or mailing it, your signature should always be included.

The last line of the cover letter should say, "Enclosures (#)". The # is the number of documents that follow the cover letter. Typically, they include your CV and references.

Summary

Of the three types of cover letter, the one most generally used is referred to as an invited cover letter. Always follow the same format for crafting cover letters. Each letter should have a *header*, an *introduction*, a *body*, *contact information*, and a *closing*. Don't forget to sign the cover letter either digitally or with a black pen.

Notes

1 Alison Doyle, "Different Types of Cover Letters," http://jobsearch.about.com/od/coverletters/a/types-of-cover-letters.htm.

4 JOB HUNTING

The job was several weeks from ending. Of course, companies almost never know exactly when a job will end. There is always something that comes up at the last minute. All the best sites, features, and artifacts are found on the last day of fieldwork. Sometimes, though, nothing turns up, and the project ends early. Either way, no one knows. You have to watch out for yourself and be prepared.

My wife and I started looking for work several weeks before the proposed end of the job. We started with Shovelbums, of course. Then we checked archaeologyfieldwork.com. Back then, they were the best options. After sending out a few curriculum vitae (CVs), we moved on to calling a few friends to see if there was space on their projects. Once we found something that somewhat corresponded to the end of our project we had to decide when to leave. Sometimes you have to leave a few days before the end just to make it to the start of the next project. That's just the nature of the business, and good employers understand that.

In many ways, finding a job today is the same as it was years ago, before the Internet. You just have to think about it differently. Before, you used to call around to friends and employers to see if they knew of any work in your area or if they knew anyone that was hiring. We do the same thing now, but, instead of using the phone, we use the Internet.

This chapter will cover the different ways of finding work in cultural resource management (CRM) archaeology. We will cover everything from good 'ol networking, to neo-traditional job posting sites, to crowd-sourced job hunting.

Networking

A useful tool for starting a job search is still just a phone call away. In some ways, it's easier to call people now than it was a few decades ago. Everyone has a cell phone and voicemail. If you have a large network of companies and colleagues, then your quickest route to employment might just be an afternoon or two on the phone.

Field Archaeologist's Survival Guide: Getting a Job and Working in Cultural Resource Management by Chris Webster pp. 33–38 ©2014 Left Coast Press, Inc. All rights reserved.

The highest paying archaeology per-diem gig I ever had came by way of a fax from Patrick H. Garrow to Cory Breternitz's Soil Systems Incorporated in Phoenix. Garrow & Associates needed staff for a big pipeline job and sent an announcement fax to other companies. Someone brought the fax out to the field for lunch one day and it was passed around and debated. – R. Joe Brandon, Shovelbums.org

In areas of the country where work is seasonal, when the snow melts there is usually a flurry of calls to the companies we worked for in the fall. If that doesn't pan out, then the next step is to start calling friends from the last project. If you still don't have a job, then you start moving out from there.

Neo-Traditional Sources

There are actually quite a few sites on the Internet where jobs are posted. Two of the most used and most popular sites are archaeologyfieldwork.com and Shovelbums.

archaeologyfieldwork.com

This website (www.archaeologyfieldwork.com) was started by Jennifer Palmer in 1996 and has been going strong ever since. On the website, you'll find job postings curated from a number of agencies—including government agencies. A big reason why archaeologyfieldwork.com is so popular is that it's free to post jobs. Any employer can post any job anytime they want to. Postings are generally up for 60 days and then deleted.

Life on the road is as insecure as it is free. Having spent seven continuous years living on the road as a shovelbum across 25 states, I know how hard it can be to know what direction to go next. – Wilbur Barrick

Other benefits of the archaeologyfieldwork.com website include a *News* forum, a *Discussion forum*, a *Résumé* forum for posting your CV, and a *Resources* page loaded with useful links. I frequently post news stories, my blog posts, and new episodes of my podcast on archaeologyfieldwork.com. Logging in is easy if you want to comment, otherwise, you can see the discussion threads and job postings without signing up.

You can find archaeologyfieldwork.com on Facebook, Twitter, and LinkedIn.

Shovelbums

This might be the most well-known website (www.shovelbums.org) just for the name alone. The collective term for an archaeology field tech in the

United States is *Shovelbum*, and you don't go long in this business without hearing that word. Founded in 1999 by R. Joe Brandon, the site currently has over 15,000 members. Brandon maintains the site as a full time job. Almost every job I've ever found came from a Shovelbums post.

One of the most convenient aspects of Shovelbums is the ability to join the mailing list. Every day I get an email with the job postings from the previous day. In the spring, when you really need a job, checking the website several times a day becomes necessary.

The quality of job postings on Shovelbums varies. Many employers seem to think that posting their company profile and buzz words matters to someone looking for work. They often forget to include details such as pay, per diem, and the job type. I still don't understand how the phrase, "pay is commensurate with experience" means anything to anyone. At least put in the pay range with the listing so someone not familiar with the regional pay scales can have an idea. It would be nice if R. Joe Brandon had a form with important fields that employers could use to post jobs. That way they wouldn't forget the information that most field techs find important.

The Shovelbums website also contains a listing of field schools that are offered around the world. If you haven't had a field school yet—which is required for most jobs—then you should take a look and find something that can benefit you down the road. It is generally not free to post a job on Shovelbums. There is a slightly complicated pricing structure listed on the website. It costs $100 to post one position from one state. As you add positions and states the cost goes up $100 for each category. For example, if you are hiring ten field techs for one project in one state then the cost for listing is $100. If you are hiring ten field techs and a crew chief for the same state the cost is $200. If you are hiring ten field techs from projects in two states, the cost is $200. There is no fee for academic postings. R. Joe Brandon says on the website that no one will be turned away from posting jobs on Shovelbums. If your company can't afford the cost, or is new and isn't generating revenue yet, he'll still let you post as long as you pay next time you need to post and when your company has a better financial standing. His ultimate goal, after all, is to keep people employed. A worthy goal, indeed. Shovelbums is on Facebook and LinkedIn.

Other Internet Job Hunting Sources

USA Jobs

Looking for a government job? The military, National Park Service, Bureau of Land Management, and the Forest Service, among others, post available positions on the USA Jobs website (www.usajobs.gov). The length of the positions can be for a certain season, term, or indefinite. In many cases, agencies are required to post jobs for a certain period of time in a forum such as USA Jobs.

It doesn't cost money to find a job on USA Jobs but it will cost you time. There is a somewhat lengthy process you have to go through in order to sign up. You have to go through the process, however, in order to apply for any jobs listed on the website.

When applying for a job on USA Jobs, your application is ranked using a points system. You get points for having certain degrees, years of experience, skills, and you even get points for being a military veteran. Many people lose out on jobs to veterans because, all other things being equal, the veterans get the extra points to push them over the top.

LinkedIn

This website (www.linkedin.com) is quickly gaining traction as a powerful resource for employers and job seekers. LinkedIn is similar to other websites, like Facebook and Google+, where you have a profile, a post stream, and groups. The difference is that you're unlikely to see a cat video posted to LinkedIn. There are other differences, but that one is the most important!

On LinkedIn, you have the ability to create a profile that details your work history, education, and publications. It is designed to be your online résumé and a place where employers can seek out new employees. You can also endorse qualifications of others, and you can solicit recommendations from your connections.

One powerful feature of LinkedIn is LinkedIn Groups. There are groups for just about every topic. Joining a group that is very active is a great way to stay on top of news, trends, and discussions related to your topic of interest. Most of my blog comments come from LinkedIn.

I've noticed that most archaeologists on LinkedIn are upper level, meaning, they are project managers, principal investigators, and company owners. There are few field techs on the website, but the number is growing. Get on LinkedIn and start networking before you graduate from college. It will benefit you in the end.

Other Resources

There are a number of other places where jobs are posted, but they aren't used by many of the local employers. Jobs are posted on About.com, Underwater Archaeology Jobs, Monster.com, and many others. Use your favorite search engine to find more resources if Shovelbums and archaeo ogyfieldwork.com don't work out for you. Something else to keep in mind is that more large engineering firms are developing cultural resources departments. These firms often have someone, or entire departments, dedicated to finding personnel. They will often post jobs on more traditional resources like Monster.com. They are also likely to post jobs on their own company websites. If you know of a large firm that you would like to work for in your area, then go to the website, and see if they've posted anything.

Crowd-Sourced Job Hunting

A relatively new phenomenon in the world of CRM archaeology is crowd-sourced job hunting. This technique is very underutilized by most archaeologists, but for the few of us that are "plugged in," it's becoming increasingly useful. First, what is *crowd-sourcing*?

Crowd-Sourcing

Websites like Twitter, Facebook, Google+, and LinkedIn all have a similar model for collecting friends and distributing bits of information to many people at once. Twitter is the easiest way to disperse a short piece of information (or a lot of information if you include a link to a website) to a massive amount of people. LinkedIn is probably the most restricted way to do it. When you post something to Twitter, it is visible to anyone monitoring your Twitter stream (which anyone can do without your knowledge) and to anyone that has followed you on Twitter. The posts, or tweets, from people you follow show up in your primary Twitter stream and are the most basic way to view information.

If you want to get more selective with your tweets you can use hashtags. A hashtag is any word or phrase (with no spaces) preceded by a "#". The usefulness of this technique is evident when searching for a term or phrase. One of the Twitter streams I have on my website (www.digtech-llc.com/blog/) contains a chronological listing of all the tweets that have "#archaeology" somewhere in the message. I also monitor the hashtags "#crmarch" and conference tags like "#SAA2014".

If your Twitter stream gets too cluttered, because you'll follow just about anyone, then you can refine your stream by using lists. Monitor a list stream the same way you watch other streams. All the tweets from the people in the list are filtered into one stream.

Google+ and Facebook have a similar functionality with hashtags. They still aren't as widely used as Twitter, however. The advantage with Google+ and Facebook is that you aren't limited to 140 characters in one post like you are with Twitter. The disadvantage of those services is that the usage doesn't come close to matching Twitter right now.

Crowd-Sourcing for Jobs

Rather than explain how I use crowd-sourcing to find jobs, let's look at a hypothetical work flow and how I would approach the situation.

While browsing the archaeology group on Facebook, I notice that someone needs a few field techs for a job in a state I'm not in or familiar with. Since it's Facebook, they are likely a friend or colleague, so I decide to comment on the thread and ask for more information. Once I have it, I share that request on my Facebook timeline where I have more friends in the business that might not be in the group. My Facebook page automatically posts to Twitter and since I'm savvy on how Twitter works I was sure to include hashtags like #archaeology and #crmarch in my Facebook post. Now, thousands of people are seeing my request for people and information. Those people will likely retweet my tweet and that will share it with their friends and so on. Meanwhile, I've posted the request on some of the groups I belong to on LinkedIn, and I've posted it on Google+. Within a few hours, suggestions start pouring in and connections can be made.

This isn't just a hypothetical situation. I've seen this happen with people and with artifact identification. A simple artifact photograph sent to Twitter with a request for identification can yield results in a very short period of time. In one instance, I had the answer to a question before I even left the site. I call this sort of crowd-sourcing Archaeology 2.0, and it is only the beginning of the future.

Summary

There are many ways to find jobs. They range from the traditional (calling around and talking to people) to the neo-traditional (searching on job posting websites) and to the more modern crowd-sourced way of posting requests on social media sites. If you're willing to travel and work anywhere, then you shouldn't have any problem finding work. The problem that most people have with finding work in CRM archaeology is that they limit their search to a small geographic area. If you want to be successful during the early years of your career, then you are going to have to learn to be flexible and move around. After you gain some experience, you can look for that cushy salaried position and start to settle down. That is, until the bottom falls out of the market, and you get laid off and have to start all over. Welcome to CRM archaeology.

5 THE INTERVIEW

My first interview took place over the phone. Many of your interviews will. It was for a job in Florida that included digging for human remains. The site's date range covered the historic period and back several thousand years. When the company owner called me, he said he was impressed by my curriculum vitae (CV) and wanted to know if I'd come down to work on the project. Impressed by my CV? I had one three-week project under my belt and that was it. However, I'd highlighted my osteology class in college on my CV before submitting it to this firm. He loved it. That was exactly what he was looking for.

I've never had a sit-down archaeology interview in the traditional sense. I've talked to potential employers in their offices, but the job was usually already mine. In cultural resource management (CRM) archaeology, you have to be prepared to do things a little differently, especially at the field technician level. Nothing is done the way it is in other professions, and you have to be prepared.

Alright. You typed up a CV, had it checked by friends and colleagues, and looked for some job postings. The perfect job came up, so you typed up a customized cover letter and sent off the email to your future employer. Now what? Many people don't realize when they get into CRM that this is not like other jobs. You likely won't be called for an actual interview unless it is a higher leadership position. If you receive a phone call for a field technician spot, they are likely offering you the job. Some companies are not very discriminating when it comes to hiring field techs. Other employers will read your CV or résumé, check your references, and then call you in for an interview. CRM companies usually stop at the "read your CV" step. In my experience they don't even really do that. Why is this?

Well, in other professions you are probably planning on being there for a while. The companies want to see you and talk to you so they can have an idea as to what they are getting themselves into. When you get to the job there will probably be a 60-90 day probationary period where they can fire you at any time. Nearly every CRM job is a probationary period, and at any point you can be fired or dismissed. In some cases you might finish out the project, but you may not be called back if they have additional work. This is a small field and everyone talks. Nearly every company I've worked for has asked my co-workers and I about possible new employees. They ask if we've ever worked with "these people" and whether we'd ever work with them again. I've seen CVs tossed in the trash without a second thought. It's brutal but a reality of our field.

So, how should you prepare for that phone call? For my first few hiring phone calls, I didn't ask many questions. I asked what my pay was going to be and where the job was taking place, but that's about it. After a few frustrating circumstances, I decided to develop my own list of questions for the employer.

Interviewing the Interviewer

After your future employer finishes telling you all about the wonders of working for their company, and they're just waiting for you to say "when do I need to be there," you pause for a second, then hit them with a barrage of your own questions. That's how modern, professional, field techs get noticed. Let's talk about what questions to ask now that you have their attention.

Pay and Per Diem

For most field techs pay and per diem are two of the most important concerns they have. However, I've started projects where some of the techs had no idea how much they were getting paid and when they were getting paid. So, the first questions on my list are about pay and per diem.

With pay, you should start by asking how much. If you think it's too low for the region you're working in, and for your experience level, then ask about the pay range. Many companies have set low and high pay rates for certain positions. Find out where you fit in that system. If you don't like where they put you, make a case for a better rate. What do you have to lose?

The other big question with pay is "when." All companies have a pay schedule. Find out when you will be getting paid because it could be a while. You might not receive a paycheck for three weeks to a month after starting the project. That's likely going to be financially stressful on most people, especially since you might not get your per diem until your first paycheck.

Now we come to per diem. Per diem is Latin for "per day". This is the money that CRM companies give for, at a minimum, food during the workday. There are many variations as to the amount and method of distribution for per diem. You need to find out what the company's policy is. Some of the common variations include cash per diem on the first day of the week or session; per diem at the end of the session; per diem at the same time as your paycheck; and per diem on a different schedule from the paycheck.

The amount of per diem is also highly variable but generally falls into two categories. You'll either get a lot or a little. You'll get usually $80 to $150 if you are responsible for your accommodations. You could get as little as $21, or less, per diem if you are just getting paid for food. When getting the higher rate, many field techs will choose to share a hotel room or camp. For many techs, per diem is used to live on over the winter when the field season ends.

Per diem will generally come in one of three forms. You could get cash at the beginning of the week or session. That's my preferred method. Most of the time, you'll get it in the form of a check either on its own schedule or with your paycheck. The third method is also a check, but you only get your per diem after turning in receipts for your food. This is the least-preferred method for receiving per diem. For reasons known only to accountants, per diem almost never comes via direct deposit.

Lodging

On the East Coast, lodging is often, but not always, double occupancy. Sometimes you can choose your roommate and sometimes you are randomly assigned to a room. I generally avoided these situations when I was single because I felt that getting treated like an adult and not a college student was key to my sanity.

The West Coast companies usually leave you to your own devices when it comes to lodging. Some companies still insist on direct billing the hotel, though. For some people, the lodging situation is an important question to ask potential employers. Others don't care. It might not really matter to you if the project is of a short duration. If you travel around in a van with all your worldly possessions stacked inside, then you likely just want a full and high per diem rate so you can stake your claim on a small patch of Bureau of Land Management land to call your own for the duration of the session.

Project Length and Future Work

Is the project slated to last two days, two weeks, or two months? Ask. It's important. Is it worth it to drive 1,000 miles for a two-week project? Depends on the project. Find out how long it's supposed to last and whether they have other projects lined up after that. Employers don't want people to quit before the project is over, and they don't like hiring new people, so they might inflate the durations of projects and tell you they have a lot of work coming up. That might be true; but they may not have permits in place, and there could be delays. I'm not saying employers are dishonest about future projects; just overly optimistic. Always have a backup plan and/or some money in the bank.

Cultural Background

I like to find out what type of project I'm going on, so I can look up information about the history and/or the region before I get there. It lets me know what types of artifacts to look for and informs me of any unique archaeological features. You could also ask the company if they can recommend any books or papers related to the project area.

The Work Day

There is a lot of variation in what employers call a workday and what they pay you for. The ideal situation from a field tech's standpoint is being paid "hotel to hotel". That means you are on the clock from the time you leave the hotel to the time you return. Find out whether overtime is authorized or whether you are on salary. Some companies don't start the clock until you get into the field or they will only pay drive-time one way. If the project area is an hour from the hotel and you aren't getting drive time, you could be giving up two hours of your day, or 20 hours during a 10-day session, for free. Of course, if the project is really awesome and interesting, it might be worth it.

Ask about the work schedule. I've worked schedules that vary from ten days on, four days off, to nine days on, five days off. There are Monday through Friday schedules, Monday through Thursday schedules, and eight on, six off schedules. Some companies pay per diem on the days off but most don't. Ask about your company's procedures.

Rain Day Policy

This might seem trivial, but in the springtime, rain days could mean the difference between a full paycheck and half of a paycheck. Companies often have a policy for rain days. Some won't pay you at all and might ask for your per diem back for that day. Others will pay you for two, four, or six hours and let you keep your per diem. Some companies will have everyone drive out to the project area to make a determination about work as a matter of policy, and others will just check the radar. This may not be a factor in your decision to join the project, but it's good to know because it usually doesn't come up until it happens.

Sick Days

Some companies will ask you to return your per diem if you call in sick. Find out what your company's policy is. Do you get health benefits after a certain period? Some bigger companies give benefits after 90 days. You don't often get on projects that last that long, but it's nice if you do.

Other Questions

You might not have to ask all these questions, and you might have to ask more questions. It all depends upon your experience level and your experience with both the company and the region. You are giving your valuable time and expertise to a project for a certain period. Be sure you know what you're getting into, and make sure you are well compensated, because without you, the project would never happen.

Summary

When you get a phone call from a potential employer in the wild world of CRM archaeology, you are likely being offered a job. At the field technician level, you are rarely called in for an interview unless you are being offered a permanent position. When you do get that call, though, have a list of questions ready for the employer. You want to make sure you know how much you're getting paid, when you're getting paid, what the per diem situation is, and the answers to many other questions. Be a professional and know what you are getting into before you get there.

SECTION 2

SHOVELBUMMING

Shovelbumming is an art, really. Unfortunately, there are very few people who understand this art. It is only through this understanding that you can be truly content with your career and your lifestyle. The next section will show you ways to enhance your experiences so you don't get frustrated and leave the field because you aren't happy. Of course, I'm not promising happiness. In the end, your level of happiness is really up to you. What I can do is show you ways to make your life easier and more familiar. It's the lack of familiarity that I often find is a reason for people getting out of cultural resource management. We're always in a different state, city, hotel room, and with different people, and it can be very unsettling if you don't know how to handle it.

None of the following tips and advice will help you unless you are really seeking a way to make this career work. Most of us, in all fields of archaeology, have a passion for what we do. It's what gets us up in the morning, and it's what makes us drive a thousand miles for a two-week gig that looks "really fun." If you don't have that passion, though, then you'll find reasons to be unhappy, and you'll bring everyone down around you. So, for the people who LOVE archaeology but are still unhappy, this section, and this book, is for you.

This section will cover the type of gear you need (chapter 6), at a minimum, to be a shovelbum. Of course, everyone has different ideas as to what they need, but everyone at some point usually needs everything in this list. Chapter 7 covers project types and is intended to give people new to the field an understanding as to what types of projects are out there. Knowing what positions are available for you in archaeology can help you define your goals and know your leadership structure. Chapter 8, Job Positions, is important for people at all levels. The section ends with chapters on lodging types (chapter 9), hotels specifically (chapter 10), a chapter on the subtle, but necessary, art of cooking on the road (chapter 11), and camping (chapter 12).

6 ESSENTIAL GEAR

My first project was an excavation in Minnesota. I owned nothing in the way of field gear. After my first day, I went to the hardware store trying to find something called a "Marshalltown" trowel. I had to go to several stores before I found one. I also bought a plumb bob, folding ruler, and a cheap compass. It turned out that I really didn't need the compass on the excavation. Who knew?

My second project was also an excavation, but that company gave every new employee a bucket full of gear, much of which you could keep when you left the project. That's how I built my excavation kit. After a few more excavations, I finally got a survey. Now I had to buy a real compass and get a backpack. I thought that any old backpack would do but quickly discovered my error. The one I bought was uncomfortable and didn't hold much.

By the time I got to Nevada, where six- to ten-mile pedestrian surveys are a dime-a-dozen, my field bag was big and light, and my gear was efficient and manageable. It only took four or five years to get to that point. Learn from my mistakes and get the right gear as soon as you can.

Now that you have a job (hopefully), and you are packing for your first road trip as a shovelbum, it's probably time to make sure you have everything you need. As you work in different parts of the country, you'll realize that you need slightly different gear choices. Of course, you'll need different gear from survey to excavation all over the country. Fortunately, excavation is mostly the same everywhere. Survey gear is mostly the same too but you can make some choices depending on where you are working.

Essential gear: Hydration pack, absolutely. Hydrate, hydrate, hydrate. Don't be a hater; be a hydrator, is my motto!

First aid kit, a good knife (folding or otherwise) or multi-tool, compass, extra batteries! – Jennifer McGuire

Field Archaeologist's Survival Guide: Getting a Job and Working in Cultural Resource Management by Chris Webster pp. 46–54 ©2014 Left Coast Press, Inc. All rights reserved.

Universal Gear Needs

Backpack

There is a lot of variation in the type of backpack you can choose, but, first you have to answer a question: one backpack or two? Everyone has some sort of backpack for survey. However, some people have a different back-pack for excavation, and many people don't have one at all. They just use a toolbox, tool bag, or any sort of container. I know someone that used a large ammunition can for an excavation toolbox.

Let's assume you're looking for a survey backpack. If you're doing survey in an area where shovel testing every 30 meters is the preferred method, then you want a medium-sized backpack. It's not crucial that it fit like a hiking backpack or that it has a lot of securing straps that go around your waste and chest. Once you start shovel testing on your transect, you'll be taking the pack off and putting it down once every 30 meters anyway. The pack's primary function is to hold your water, lunch, artifact bags, and any other supplies you might need. So, get something light and efficient. Make sure, though, that it has good, thick, zippers—sealed zippers would be even better—because your pack is going to spend a lot of time on the ground and in the dirt; so it's going to get quite dirty. Big zippers work bet-ter than small zippers when they get inevitably dirty and sandy. The small zippers get chunks of sand in the teeth and stop working.

Keeping your backpack dry is just as important as keeping yourself dry. Many backpacks won't keep their contents dry during a surprise rain shower. While you're running back to the truck, all your paperwork will get wet. Some packs have a built-in rain cover that secures away in its own pocket. You can also buy rain covers in various sizes. Don't get one that's too big or too small, or rain could get in.

The best affordable rain suit I've ever used is the raincoat and pants made by Helly Hansen. It's not breathable, but why waste time wearing rain gear if it's too hot for you to just roll with quick-dry Patagonia, Capeline, or Under Armor? Helly Hansen will keep water and wind out, period. You just need to stay away from cats and blackberry hedges. – Bill White

One of the single most valuable pieces of equipment is a good, lightweight, rain jacket. – Justin Dunnavant

If you're working in a region where you'll be doing mostly pedestrian survey, such as in the Southwest or the Great Basin, then a lightweight hiking daypack is in order. Get one with a rigid aluminum frame insert and thick, padded waist straps. The waist straps help take the weight off your shoulders. When you're doing survey in the desert, it's common to walk eight to twelve miles a day, and you're going to need a pack that is both comfortable and able to hold five to eight liters of water, your lunch, and your recording supplies.

I'd suggest getting your first pack somewhere with a generous return policy. You can try the pack on at the store, and get it properly fitted, but the only way you're going to know if it's going to work out is if it still feels comfortable on mile ten of a long day of survey. A popular, but not always least expensive, store for packs is REI. If you are a co-op member, which only costs $20 for life, then you can return purchased and used items to the store. Check their website for current return policies. If needed, you can return a pack after a session and get a different one.

Water retention in the pack is important to consider. If you're working on a shovel-testing crew, you may just have water in containers inside your pack. However, out in the desert and in places where you are walking for hours at a time without stopping, you'll want a pack with a water reservoir and a drinking tube. Sometimes stopping to take a drink is not an option, and you'll want to be able to do it on the move. Most, if not all, daypacks come with a compartment to put a water reservoir, and some actually come with the reservoir installed. Make sure the pack will hold at least a three-liter reservoir. Those are the most common large size. There are larger sizes, but most packs can't hold them, and you'll need every bit of it in the summer time. I carry a three-liter reservoir and an extra two-liter reservoir that I refill the primary one with when it's empty. Over an eight-hour day, you should be drinking at least five liters of water, and maybe more, depending on the environmental factors and your own physiology.

Finally, your pack should have a lot of pockets. You'll appreciate the organization when you are trying to find a pencil to replace the one you dropped down a mineshaft. If your pack is for shovel testing, a separate compartment for artifact bags is nice to have. Also, if your pack doesn't come with one, you might look into a rain cover. Nothing is worse than a soaking wet pack that you have to hump all the way to the truck.

Compass

A compass is one of the most basic tools that every archaeologist needs. In areas where shovel testing is the primary survey method, compasses are essential. After every shovel test, a compass is used to sight in the next location. In the west, and other areas where pedestrian survey is the way of the land, a compass is used to keep you on your transect. Of course, GPS is quickly taking over basic survey functions. Often, you are following a Universal Transverse Mercator (UTM) (see chapter 13) northing or easting rather than a compass heading. Still, though, you'll use a compass while recording a site to mark the orientation of features and photographs.

There are a number of qualities and types of compasses. There are a few attributes, in particular, that you should look for in any compass. One of the most important characteristics a compass should have is the ability to adjust the declination. Sites are recorded and transects are walked relative to true north. However, a simple compass only points true north in a couple spots on the globe. Everywhere else it points magnetic north. What you need to know right now is that if you are working anywhere other than where the declination is zero degrees, you'll want to be able to adjust your compass. You can always offset your heading to compensate for the magnetic declination, but that can get confusing and who wants to do math in the field? Your compass should also have a sighting mirror. That's the mirror that you see when you fold open the compass. To use a compass, hold it away from your body at arm's length to avoid interference from your own electromagnetic fields and any metal on your body. When held at arm's length, it is nearly impossible to see the compass needle. Adjust the mirror to allow you to see the needle.

Finally, one last attribute that I prefer on a compass is one-degree increments on the bezel. Cheaper compasses have five-degree increments, and some have two-degree increments. I've often had to record an angle down to the single degree. Why guess between a few degrees? Just get a compass with one-degree increments and save yourself some trouble.

Extra Compass Attributes

When you buy a fancy compass, it can come with some fun extra features. Some of these features include map scales on the edges, a ruler on one edge, a clinometer for determining the heights of distant objects and the steepness of hillsides, emergency medical information in the form of water-safe cards, and a rubberized protective case that sometimes can be used as an eraser. You're going to spend a lot of time with your compass. Buy one you'll be happy with.

Trowel

Most archaeologists cherish their trowels more than they would cherish their first-born child. Other gear comes and goes, but the trowel often stays for decades. Through repeated sharpening and use, it is soon whittled down to a fraction of its original size. There are two primary types of trowels and generally only one that most people get.

My detailed "Benchmark" and "Gazetteer" state maps were among my most important gear. They were practical; they allowed me to adapt to new regions by showing the possibilities for camping, navigation, and exploration. - Wilbur Barrick

The most common trowel is the pointed trowel. They come in various lengths. Some have straight sides while others have curved sides. I prefer a straight-sided, pointing trowel of about 4.5 inches in length. The next most common type of trowel is the square—or margin—trowel. The margin trowel is essentially shaped like a rectangle with straight sides all around. The margin trowel is useful in soils that are soft and where getting those walls straight and corners to 90 degrees is a challenge. They're also useful if you don't have a lot of rocks and roots in your soil. Pointed trowels are useful for picking out rocks and digging around roots. It's probably best to buy one of each and keep them sharp!

Ask any archaeologist in the United States what kind of trowel they have, and nine times out of ten they will say "Marshalltown." It's certainly not the only type of trowel in the country, but it is the most trusted and respected and has been used by archaeologists for many years. You can buy Marshalltown trowels in some hardware stores or online.

Clipboard

For most phases and types of archaeology, you will likely need a clipboard. For some companies in the southeast, I've just used Write-In-The-Rain field notebooks instead of a clipboard, but you'll still want to get one. There are three basic types. The simplest clipboard is a flat piece of cardboard, wood, or plastic with a clip at the top. It is virtually guaranteed that your paperwork will be all but destroyed if you use one of these. Some companies will buy these clipboards in bulk and issue them to unprepared field techs on the off chance they don't have one of their own. If you need to use one of these types of clipboards, at least put a rubber band around the end to keep your papers from blowing in the wind. The thicker the band you use, the less likely your paper is to rip. You can get elastic bands from craft stores to wrap around your clipboard. I have one around the clipboard portion of my metal clipboard.

The next type of clipboard is an enclosed plastic one. There are a few variations but most of them consist of a plastic clipboard with an internal storage area. Some have a separate storage compartment at the bottom for pencils and other supplies. The clip is usually on the outside of the unit, and the inside is for storage of extra or finished paperwork. You'll still want some sort of strap at the bottom for keeping your papers on the outside from blowing around and getting ripped or lost.

The final type of clipboard is made of aluminum and comes in several different forms. Some have a clip on the outside, some on the inside, and some have a clip on both the inside and outside. All have internal storage for extra or finished paperwork. The metal clipboards vary in thickness from one-half inch to two inches with storage for a lot of paperwork. You'll still want a strap to keep paperwork from blowing away. The metal clipboard has its drawbacks. They can get cold in the winter and hot in the summer. Sometimes the clipboard is so hot that it's difficult to handle. I always try to put mine in the shade or under my pack when I set it down. Of course, some people don't even use clipboards and choose to go the more "hi-tech" route.

> My favorite field gear is my laptop which I can use to look up historical maps (principally BLM GLO) after I come across historical structures or buildings. – Bill White

Pick a clipboard that suits your circumstances. If you want lightweight but less durable, choose a plastic one. If you want it to last longer and are OK with a little more weight, go with the aluminum variety. Unless you are a crew chief, you can probably get away with one of the smaller aluminum ones. Choose wisely because you're likely going to have it for a while.

Orange Vest

A number of archaeology projects take place on active construction sites or in areas that will soon be construction sites. Orange vests are usually required in those areas. Sometimes archaeologists, the smart ones, wear vests during hunting season to avoid getting mistaken for a homeless ungulate. Often, a company will provide you with a foul smelling, ill fitting safety vest. If you're going to be wearing a safety vest most of the time, you'll be better off just buying your own. Buy a lightweight one with several pockets. You don't want it to be too thick and warm because you'll likely wear the same one all year. In the winter, you want it to be big enough to wear over multiple layers of cold weather gear.

> I consider my cloth handkerchief for wiping my nose essential, as well as the larger ones that I use to cover my neck, chest, hair, and ears. They are my natural sunscreen. I use clothing instead of lotion to protect my skin. People may look at me weird, but I find it comfortable (even in 100+ degree weather) and that it works better than sunscreen. No need to reapply, no greasy feeling, no stinging when it gets in your eyes. – Jennifer McGuire

Vests come in generally two colors: safety yellow and blaze orange. Most vests people wear are orange. Some companies in the Great Basin require a particular color. Ask the company you're working for if any of their clients have a vest color requirement. Some clients also require reflective tape on the vest, and not all vests come with it. Check your client's requirements and either buy one with reflective tape, or do what I did, and sew some tape onto the vest you already have or want. You'll have more options if you buy a vest without tape and add it later.

Hard Hat

Generally, when you have to wear a vest, you also have to wear a hard hat. A hard hat is required on all active mining sites. If you work in the West, prepare to wear a sweaty hard hat provided by your company or by the mine. I don't know too many techs that own a hard hat, but it's a good idea to find one that fits well. Hard hats can be purchased for $6-$80. The cheap ones are just as good as the expensive ones. Often, the only difference is style and color. A good fitting hardhat can mean the difference between miserable survey and a tolerable one. You can also just buy your own inserts and hang them inside a company issued hard hat. Then, you only have to work in your own sweat, not someone else's.

Munsell Soil Color Book

This item is for the serious archaeologist. Munsell soil color books are used throughout the world to identify soil colors using a standard definition. Usually, the company you're working for will either have one person that is reading the Munsell values for the crew, or the project, or, they'll give everyone that needs one a Munsell book. If you are shovel testing or excavating, then you'll be using a Munsell book often. The full Munsell book is expensive. Price varies depending upon the options you choose. Individual pages can be purchased from some websites and that might be all you need. A few techs out there that just have two or three of the most common pages, and they generally get by with that.

Excavation Tools

Take a look at ten different dig kits from ten different field technicians, and you won't find the exact same things in each one. Everyone has his or her preferences. There are a few things, however, that each dig kit should have.

Line Level

Line levels are cheap. They are generally either aluminum or plastic. The aluminum ones have tabs that can bend over the string. The tabs can eventually cut the string, which can be troublesome. Plastic line levels won't cut the string, and they slide easily. Look around and find one that suits your needs. If you're on an excavation, look at others on the site, and see what you like and what you don't like. They usually cost less than $5, so you can shop around and maybe buy a few.

Tape Measure and/or Two-Meter Folding Rule

A line level isn't very useful if you don't have something to measure depth with. Most archaeologists have a measuring tape and a two-meter folding rule. The measuring tape should be at least two meters long and have metric and standard measurements. Historic artifacts and features are usually recorded in feet and inches, while prehistoric features are recorded using metric measurements. Also, most excavation units are excavated using metric measurements. You won't have much need for a tape that measures more than three meters, so keep the weight in your kit down, and only get what you need.

A folding two-meter ruler is great for excavations. The ability to measure the depth of your unit with a stiff ruler could make a difference when you are trying to be accurate to the centimeter. A thick, metal tape measure will do the same thing, but most people use the wooden folding rules. Tape measures can bend which makes it difficult to measure the depth of a unit down to the centimeter. It's difficult to find one that is measured in meters and you might have to look online.

Brushes

Many archaeologists have cobbled together a set of brushes that they've acquired over the years and modified to suit their needs. Look for a quality set of brushes with their own carrying case and that will ensure you can always find one. The brushes should be of good enough construction so they don't leave fine hairs behind. Brushes should be somewhat stiff so they can move dust and dirt efficiently.

Chopsticks

I'm always on the lookout for a good set of chopsticks when I go to an Asian restaurant. Chopsticks are great for doing detailed, small, excavation work when there is material that you don't want to scratch or etch with a metal tool. I have a set of different sizes of chopsticks that I've whittled down to different shapes that suit my needs. Also, since they are easy to shape quickly with a knife, I keep a few that are untouched and can be shaped into whatever I need in a few minutes.

Dental Picks

Commonly used to remove hardened material from artifacts, and to excavate delicate items in a solidified matrix, dental picks are often found in a field technician's dig kit. You can ask your dentist to hang on to their old ones for a while and then go ask for them. Usually, they'll give them to you. Some dentists don't like to hang on to old dental tools because they are a hazard, and they don't have anywhere to store them. Ask around, and there's likely to be at least one dentist that will supply you with dental picks. Of course, in some areas, you'll never use one. In the southeast, where everything is buried in sand, a dental pick isn't very useful. Also, be careful when removing the matrix around an artifact with a dental pick. They are sharp and will easily scratch or otherwise damage the artifact.

Summary

There are quite a few things you'll likely buy for an excavation, but these are the basics that virtually everyone has. Also, we didn't cover an excavation bag or container for your kit because there are just too many choices. Find something that is portable, convenient, and that will withstand the test of time.

7 TYPES OF PROJECTS

My field school and my first three projects were excavations. I wasn't sure there was another type of field project until I landed a shovel-testing survey in south-central Florida. We were digging 50-cm-square shovel tests in old rows of sugar cane fields. That's central Florida in July and August. Not the best experience. The alligators and wild boars kept us on our toes, though.

When I finally got to Utah we were doing six- to ten-mile pedestrian surveys. That was quite a shock, at first. Getting used to the altitude and the distances was rough. We worked ten days on and four days off. By the end of the session, you needed four days just for the blisters to heal. Proper boots, socks, and clothing are essential. The type of gear you need is dependent upon the type of project.

Throughout the country, there are variations on the four types of projects you are likely to encounter. There are slightly different terms for the various phases of archaeology, depending on the state and region you are working in. Generally, the four types of cultural resource management (CRM) archaeology are: survey, testing, mitigation, and monitoring. Let's discuss them in order since the development of a property will often involve all of these phases in that order.

Survey

Survey, in some shape or form, is usually the first phase of a project (Figure 7.1). It can be as simple as one person checking likely locations for archaeological sites (reconnaissance survey) and as complicated as a 300-mile, 200-meter wide corridor stretching across several mountain ranges (linear survey). There is also large block survey where you walk long transects from one side of the block to the other, turn around, and come back. In many areas, there are very small surveys for cell tower locations or other types of antennas that can be as small as 30-meters in diameter or less. There are surveys in many areas of the West that have very specific project area geometry for access roads and pads for geothermal, and other types (e.g., oil and natural gas exploration), of wells. In small areas where a high

Field Archaeologist's Survival Guide: Getting a Job and Working in Cultural Resource Management by Chris Webster pp. 55–63 ©2014 Left Coast Press, Inc. All rights reserved.

FIGURE 7.1: Survey in north-central Utah.

amount of subsurface historical artifacts are expected, a metal detecting survey is often performed.

> When I encounter people while doing survey, I usually tell them we are conducting environmental studies for the project . . . I do it more to keep people from following us around to figure out where the archaeological sites are (although, the people who would be most interested in that knowledge often know many of the locations already). – Jeffrey Baker

In areas with high amounts of soil deposition, survey usually includes shovel testing (Figure 7.2) or some other type of subsurface testing (e.g., posthole or auger testing). A typical shovel-testing survey will include transects that are 30 m wide with shovel tests placed 30 m apart. Some states have low, medium, and high probability areas that will change the shovel-testing interval depending on the priority. The minimum size of the shovel test varies by state. In some states, shovel tests are excavated to approximately 30 cm in diameter, while other states prefer 50-cm-square shovel tests. Check with your company, and make sure you know what the requirements and recording standards are. Shovel testing and recording requirements are good things to ask about on the initial phone call with the company.

FIGURE 7.2: A typical shovel test. This one is from coastal Washington State.

Be aware of telling people you're an archaeologist on survey.

Know the political climate of the area you are working in and consider your security and the security of your crew.

I have seen crew members attract stalkers who'd collect a little intel from one person, a little from another . . . and soon know all the info on their target's housing, schedule, you name it.

Depending on where you are working, it's not always smart to let on that you are an archaeologist. In the early 1990s, being marked an archaeologist in the Moab area caused more than a couple techs to be roughed up behind a bar. In those areas it's better to tell folks that you are doing a "survey", avoid wearing the funny archaeology tee shirts, or just avoid the shady bars altogether. – Jim Christensen

In places like the Great Basin where there is little to no soil deposition, a pedestrian survey is performed (Figure 7.3). This generally entails a walk-over of the area utilizing the 30-meter transect interval. Some companies prefer to survey the entire area prior to recording any sites so they can tell the client what to expect when site recording does begin. Other companies will record sites as they find them. Again, ask your company what their policy is for that project. Some companies differentiate an early phase of a project, however, I'm not going into detail because you are not likely to be involved. That early phase is called a literature, or, record search. Before

FIGURE 7.3: Pedestrian survey in the Great Basin, central Nevada.

crews enter the field, the company checks local and state records for historic documents pertaining to the project area and for previously recorded sites that they need to be aware of.

Testing

Occasionally, sites will go straight into the excavation or mitigation phase following a survey; however, a few will go into what's called Phase II in some parts of the US and simply site testing in other regions. Site testing can include any number of excavation strategies. The chosen strategy depends upon the type of site that is being tested, the depositional context, and the goals of the research design.

Several possible excavation types are involved with site testing. The first step is usually some sort of intense subsurface testing. That could include close-interval shovel testing (5 m grid or less sometimes) or auger testing. The results of the close-interval investigation can yield information that leads to test pit excavations. These are usually 1 × 1 m test units (they could be larger and trench-like as well). Site testing can also include backhoe trenches and block scrapes (backhoe or shovel) to look at the stratigraphy and to locate features.

On a project flush with cash, site testing can include various electronic methods. These could be anything ranging from metal detecting to ground-penetrating radar (GPR). Most CRM companies will not use this type of equipment either because they don't have it or because the budget is stretched too thin. More efficient work procedures and efficient use of technology could free up some money for these activities, but that is a subject for another book.

Mitigation

If a site is still eligible for listing on the National Register of Historic Places after the previous phases are complete, it will then transition into the mitigation phase (Figure 7.4). Mitigation does not always involve excavation. Sometimes the words are used interchangeably. Mitigation refers to the plan that will be used to address the preservation of the site. Preservation could include a reroute of the project area or a fence that would result in completely avoiding the site. It could also include simply paving over a deeply buried site. Data are not lost in that case. The site is simply preserved for a very long time. Often, though, mitigation does involve some sort of large-scale excavation.

Block excavation takes many forms but often has one goal: to locate features. Sometimes an excavation plan will have technicians "chase" features by opening units in specific directions based on artifact quantities or some other notable criteria resulting in a crossword puzzle-like shape. Other times, a block could be simply a large square or rectangle with 1 × 1 m units systematically excavated. The type and the depth of the excavation

FIGURE 7.4: Block excavation in central Nevada. This block measured 10 × 10 m², so units were excavated in a checkerboard pattern to help technicians keep out of each other's way.

are determined by the type of site that is expected to be there, the types of features expected, and usually by the landform and soil stratigraphy.

Screening

As I said above, my first field project was an excavation. Everyone knew that I was new to the field, but I think because I was 30 years old meant that people thought I had some sort of knowledge of things without ever having done them before. Case in point: screening (Figure 7.5).

We were excavating in partners and my first job was screener. I didn't want to seem like I didn't know what I was doing, so I asked very few questions. Since I didn't really know how to screen, or even how to operate the standing shaker screens, I waited until someone else was in the screening area. When someone went up to the screening area, I took my buckets up and watched them closely.

There are several ways to put dirt in a screen. Some people, if the bucket wasn't filled too high, can balance the standing screen on one thigh and then lift the bucket up into it. Then, you tip the bucket over, put it next to you on the ground, and use it as a table for artifacts. Another way to load a screen is to pour the dirt into the screen while it is on the ground. Then, after you tip the bucket over behind you a few feet back (when you lift the screen you'll step back a few steps), you lift the screen. You can do this in

FIGURE 7.5: The backdirt pile and screening area for my first CRM job. This is in northwestern Minnesota.

a couple steps. First, grab the handles and put a foot on the cross-piece of wood at the base of the legs, if there is one. Sometimes there isn't. I wouldn't advise this method unless the cross-piece is low to the ground and the screen is light. Otherwise, you'll break the wood. If there isn't a low, sturdy cross-piece, then place your foot at the base of one of the legs. Now, lift up on the handles while you brace the screen with your foot.

After you raise the screen make sure to put yourself into a comfortable position before shaking it. This will help with your balance. Also, remove any roots, large rocks, and other large, non-artifacts, before shaking. Shake the screen either rapidly back and forth, or, with a swinging motion that allows the dirt to hit the back wall of the screen. This allows the dirt to break up naturally. Your method depends on the amount and type of soil you have in your screen.

Once most of the material is through the screen, you can begin looking for artifacts. Start by removing any obvious artifacts. In some regions, the screen could be loaded with pottery or flakes, and you'll have your work cut out for you. There are many methods for searching through a screen for artifacts, and they all work. My method is to start with the material at the back of the screen away from the handles. Then, I balance the screen on my thigh and use both hands to pull material toward me, spreading it out in the middle as I do so. Collect material with no artifacts near your body, by the handles, while keeping un-searched material at the back. The middle is for looking for artifacts. Once all the material has been looked over, I shake the screen a few more times placing the material at the back again. I then *quickly* go through the screen again to make sure nothing was missed.

Screens that are hung on tripods from a central chain, or rope, are used in much the same way (Figure 7.6). Just make sure you don't knock the screen out of the way with your bucket while you pour the dirt in. You wouldn't be the first one in CRM to dump a bucket of unscreened dirt into the backdirt pile. Just do the ethical thing and shovel as much of it as you can back into the screen. Make a note on the artifact bag that mentions the unscreened dirt was in the backdirt pile. If an artifact were found that was missed and was sitting in the backdirt pile, you wouldn't want it getting misinterpreted as coming from your unit at the level you're digging. The artifact could be from another part of the site at a different level. It's best to let your supervisors know of your mistake rather than jeopardizing the interpretation of the site.

Monitoring

The final phase of a project is usually monitoring. Monitoring is often performed by one person that works with the construction crews as they

FIGURE 7.6: Tripod screens in central Nevada.

are disturbing the ground. Monitoring is done when sites are expected in an area but weren't found during the other phases. It can also take place when a large site is very near the area being disturbed to ensure that the construction doesn't uncover any additional material or destroy existing parts of the site. When you are monitoring you are on the schedule of the construction company so a lot of waiting is often involved. It's a good time to get some reading done. However, be careful and try to get a sense of the attitude of the people with whom you're working. If you're constantly off by yourself reading during down times, then some of them might not bother to call you over when they have questions. Who wants to talk to the snooty scientists? Not those guys.

There are a number of reasons for monitoring to occur. What you need to know is that if you are asked to monitor, you are the representative for the company on that site. You have control over what happens from that point. Anything that is found has to be recorded by you as quickly as possible, or the construction has to stop so officials and your company can be notified. It all depends upon what is found and whether they can work around it or not.

Summary

The four basic project types are *survey, testing, mitigation,* and *monitoring.* These project types go by various names and acronyms depending upon what part of the country you are working in. There are differences in how each of the project types are performed across the country. The fact remains, though, that most properties will go through some or all of these phases prior to construction, and you need to be aware of them.

I could certainly be taken to task for not mentioning terms like "class III" and "inventory" but like I said above, there is a lot of variation in terminology and methodology. It would be beyond the scope of this book to detail the specific terms used in every state and region. It would also be virtually impossible as a lot of states do not have that type of information online and would have to be contacted directly. My hope is that this chapter gives the novice field tech a brief introduction as to the types of projects they can expect to encounter as they travel around our diverse country.

8 JOB POSITIONS

For the first few years of my career, I spent my time figuring out how to be the best archaeological field technician that I could be. I'm driven to move up in whatever profession I'm in, so I was always trying to figure out how I could either emulate or exceed the capabilities of my crew chiefs and project managers. Sometimes I was resented for this, and sometimes I was promoted.

There are only four basic positions in archaeology. These positions can be called a variety of titles ranging from archaeologist II to senior scientist. The engineering firms that are starting to take over archaeology have their own position naming conventions, and they don't adhere to traditional titles. Although the names may be different, the positions of field technician, crew chief, project manager, and principal investigator usually have the same responsibilities.

Field Technician

The field technician is the most basic, and most important, job position within archaeology. They aren't responsible for the budget, for talking to clients, or for writing the report. They are responsible, however, for identifying artifacts and sites, recording sites, and for generating all of the materials that will eventually produce the final report. With just a college degree and a field school, a field technician is expected to be an expert in all aspects of what they are asked to do. It's a staggering amount of information, and the best field techs are constantly learning new skills and new techniques. In a single season, you could be asked to record pueblos in the Southwest, mining complexes in the Great Basin, and teepee rings in the upper Midwest.

Some people choose to remain a field tech for the duration of their careers. They find it to be a position with the least amount of responsibility but with the greatest potential for travel and adventure. I agree with the latter but not the former. I think that as a field tech, you have the greatest responsibility of all the positions described in this chapter. It's your responsibility to recognize an artifact or feature on survey. The crew chief can't see everything and is watching her/his own transect. You have to know what you're doing, and you have to be confident in that knowledge.

The same is true for excavation projects. I've known more than a few people that have blown through features with their shovels—I'm probably one of them—and didn't know they'd even done it. Most of the time, the crew chief would come over and notice only the last part of an ephemeral feature as it was scraped up and thrown into the bucket. Knowing what to expect when you get to a job and what artifacts and features you're likely to find is critical to being a good scientist, archaeologist, and field technician. When you feel like you are master of your domain, you can start pushing for crew chief.

Crew Chief

The crew chief is the next link in the chain of command and has the ultimate responsibility over a field crew. Often, the crew chief has to be the judge and jury on whether something is a true feature, a site, or just an anomaly. The crew chiefs really are expected to know everything out there, and they should be familiar with all different types of artifacts and features that could be encountered within the project area.

Being the only company representative in the field makes the crew chief the point of contact for clients and landowners as well. Sometimes the crew chief is as much of a diplomat as they are a leader. Soothing the tensions between landowners and their company is a daily part of the job in some areas.

When a site is recorded, it is the field technicians that do most of the recording. The crew chief, however, is ultimately responsible for the content on the site forms. The project manager or principal investigator will come to the crew chief when there is a problem. A good crew chief will train her crew members in all of the positions on the crew. If someone is sick, or for some reason can't do what they normally do, someone else will have to do it. The positions on a Western field crew typically include a photographer, mapper, an artifact inventory person, and the crew chief. Not everyone is comfortable with the latest submeter Global Positioning System devices, and not everyone can take a picture that is report quality. That being said, everyone can be trained. I always try to make sure that everyone on the crew gets the opportunity to work every position and gets to learn all the facets of a well-run crew. Smart, and educated, employees are more efficient and have a better attitude and understanding of the project.

CHAPTER 8

Project Manager

In most companies, the project manager is the person that is at the top of the chain of command for a project. The principal investigator usually gives the initial details of a project to the project manager, and it's the project manager's job to contact clients, land owners, agency representatives, and to hire crew members. The project manager is also responsible for writing the report.

Sometimes, the project manager will go into the field. When the company is short-handed, or when it's just how they do things, the project manager can also lead a crew. It's common for one person to wear many hats in cultural resource management (CRM), especially when jobs are lean, and money is tight.

The project manager is typically the first position in CRM archaeology were a master's degree is required. Many companies and agencies require a master's degree in order to be permitted or to oversee projects. Sometimes, however, a person that has been with a company for a long time, and really knows their stuff, can be promoted to project manager. That person is likely stuck in that position with that company unless they want to move down the ladder when they get a new job with another firm. If you don't have the educational credentials for a position, then you'll usually start at the bottom regardless of how much experience you have.

If you want to eventually manage projects, the best course of action is to get a master's degree. If there is a program in the region you're working in that suits your needs, apply for it. Otherwise, try to find a CRM program somewhere in the US. There are a few programs that are not region specific and will teach you how to be a better archaeologist. Those programs typically cover laws and regulations, geophysical techniques, and theory. It might be fun to study an obscure pottery type from a single site for three to five years, but if you want a career in CRM, a narrow thesis focus might not be that much of a help to you.

Principal Investigator

Principal investigator is often the highest position, aside from owner of the company, a CRM archaeologist can attain. The owner of the company is often also the principal investigator in smaller firms. The principal investigator has absolute authority and ultimate responsibility over every aspect of the project. In many cases, the principal investigator doesn't write any of the report. That is left up to the project manager. The principal investigator's name, however, is often still on the front of the report. When the client decides to sue the firm, it is the principal investigator that will be in court, regardless of what the charges are. Principal investigators in CRM archaeology have a minimum of a master's degree. Many principal investigator's that came into the field in the late 1970s and early 1980s have PhDs. A principal investigator is typically very invested in the company. They may have worked there for many years and likely know the owners, if they aren't themselves the owner. Many firms only have one principal investigator that signs off on all the projects and who brings in new projects (business development).

The primary responsibility of a principal investigator in a small firm is to talk to clients and bring in new work. This is known as business development. If you like being a field archaeologist and doing survey and excavation, then being a principal investigator is not for you. If you like schmoozing with clients, talking on the phone, and writing proposals, then go for it. In larger firms with larger bank accounts, principal investigators might have the time to do pure research and to write papers that are published and/or are presented at conferences.

Additional Positions

There are two positions that are only found in firms with laboratories. Those positions are the lab technician and the lab manager. The lab technician is responsible for cleaning artifacts, labeling artifacts, identifying artifacts, and bagging artifacts—basically, most of the work in the lab. The lab manager is the person that has overall responsibility for the quality and quantity of work produced by the lab. Often, the lab manager is the lab technician as well.

Summary

There are four basic positions in CRM archaeology. They include the field technician, the crew chief, project manager, and the principal investigator. Although these positions might have different titles at different companies, they usually have the same responsibilities. Find out what the leadership structure is at your company and do your best to move to the top. Good luck!

9 LODGING

Over the years, I've stayed in a five-star hotel, an eighteenth-century bed and breakfast, a three-story beach house on the Atlantic Ocean, a ranch house near Chaco Canyon in New Mexico, a townhouse in Utah, and in so many small motels and hotels that it's difficult to keep track. During 2008, my wife and I spent over 300 days in hotel rooms. That's living on the road. Before I went to graduate school, we spent over two months in our tent at a motel/RV park in Northern California.

Lodging is one of the most important aspects to life as a shovelbum or as a person working any profession that requires a lot of travel. Your housing situation can make or break your attitude, and you really have a lot of control over it. My wife and I once spent three months in the same hotel room. By the time we left, we had stuff all over that room! It took a while just to pack everything up and put it back the way we found it. Personalizing the hotel room helped us stay sane and have a sense of ownership and belonging. It felt like OUR room, not some sterile hotel room in central Nevada.

The following steps complete your journey to be a cultural resource management (CRM) archaeologist: you wrote a curriculum vitae (CV) and a cover letter; you applied for a job(s); and you had your interview and accepted a position. Now the fine logistics of being a traveling archaeologist begin.

There are many ways in which people live and work while on the road, and the method you choose often depends upon the amount of per diem you get. Some live as cheaply as possible by camping or sleeping in their cars. While others stay in various types of hotel/motels, and still others have vans or RVs to travel and sleep in. The choice depends largely upon the company you are working for and the region you're working in.

Company Hotel

There are very few times when I worked as a crew member where I was responsible for booking my own hotel. But, if you are, one thing to keep in mind is that the rates for an entire week (particularly if you are there for multiple weeks) are often cheaper than daily rates for five

Field Archaeologist's Survival Guide: Getting a Job and Working in Cultural Resource Management by Chris Webster pp. 68–74 ©2014 Left Coast Press, Inc. All rights reserved.

days. Also, calling a hotel or motel, rather than booking on the Internet, can garner lower rates, particularly if the project is long term.
– Jeffrey Baker

Companies approach the lodging question in various ways. On the East Coast, I've generally seen companies chose and pay for a hotel for you. You have no choice of where to stay or whom to stay with. Sometimes you will get your own room, and sometimes you will be paired up with a roommate of your choosing (especially couples). Often, you won't get a choice.

Don't mention you're an archaeologist when reserving a hotel room.

I cannot tell you how many times I have heard "We don't rent rooms to archaeologists anymore", or gotten the sense that they aren't giving me the best rates because of past problems, issues, muddy towels, dead things in refrigerators, etc.

Take advantage of the fact you are on a Federal project. Contractors qualify for government rates that might be lower than regular hotel rates.

Boxes that can take a padlock are good, too, for storing valuables. Been ripped off by more than a couple housekeepers.

If your hotel arrangements are booked only for work days, not weekends or between sessions, talk to your crew and see who wants to go in on a storage unit. If you are a 24/7 shovelbum, it pays off to not be lugging stuff around with you between jobs. Lots of them are cheap, like $40 a month, and the convenience and security are worth the extra cost.

Use credit cards, but be sure to pay them off with your per diem. This will build your credit, but won't force you to use your own cash to subsidize company operations.

– Jim Christensen

When sharing a hotel room:

Ask before you touch anything that is not yours. Ask if they would like the shower first when you get back from the field. Ask how they feel about the TV. I almost never turn it on if I'm alone, so having it on first thing in the morning as well as in the afternoon and at night . . . got annoying for me. So, just be aware of your roommate's personal preferences and try to be respectful of them. – Jennifer McGuire

So far in my archaeological career, I've stayed in some interesting places. While working in New Mexico near Chaco Canyon, a firm put us up in a rented ranch house fifty miles from the nearest town. There were five of us in the house, and there were an additional fifteen people in several trailers outside. The house had its good points, such as the massive stone fireplace and all the wood we could burn. The water wasn't drinkable though, and we had to make regular trips into town to fill water containers. That was our cost, too.

We once did a project in North Carolina where the company rented a three-story beach house on the Atlantic Coast. I was a crew chief and had the master bedroom with its own bathroom and walk-in closet. For a project in Virginia, our company put us up in an eighteenth century, historic bed and breakfast. It was the off-season for the business, so we had the place to ourselves. Unfortunately, the cook was on vacation too! We were doing a survey of the shoreline of a large lake and traveled around it in a large pontoon boat that we parked at the dock owned by the bed and breakfast. The best part, though, was the free Ms. PacMan arcade game in the recreation room by the dock. The little things keep you going. Most of the time, though, you'll be in a one to two star hotel just trying to survive.

> Never, ever let someone else pay for your motel room on the basis of price alone. I'll never forget spending a night in my clothes and waking up with a sheep pushing its head through the screen on the window. We reassured our intern that this was what 'the field' was ALL ABOUT. Her first project and she already had a real story! A flock of chickens walked into her 'room.' - John Dougherty

Lodging on Your Own

On the West coast and in the Great Basin, I've generally seen companies just give you a high per diem and let you choose your own lodging (Figure 9.1).

FIGURE 9.1: Camping in southern Utah.

On one of my past projects, there were people camping in their cars, people in hotel rooms, a couple in an RV, and a guy that just slept in his van on Bureau of Land Management (BLM) land.

Camping

There are special considerations if you plan to camp (Figure 9.2). Camping across much of the West is free on BLM land or in free BLM campgrounds. Often, there is no security and no camp host, so you will likely have to pack up your campsite every morning. If you travel with few possessions and are an early riser, then this might be an option for you. Finding a campground with a camp host or paying to camp in an RV park will provide the security (and often showers and internet) to leave your camp intact during the workday.

Camping styles vary widely across the profession. I've seen everything from small, one-person backpacking tents to canvas teepees and everything in between. I worked with a tech that liked to just string up a hammock between a couple trees and call it a night.

I generally don't travel light when I camp. It started because my wife and I were traveling and working together. We were living on the road for about a year and wanted all the comforts of home in our tent. So, I bought a tent large enough to fit a queen-sized air mattress and all our stuff. During periods of bad weather, we used to strap the mattress against the wall of the tent and bring in our reclining camping chairs. We'd set up a table between us, and sometimes a heater, and watch movies on the laptop. My wife has since changed careers (I'm sure it's because she didn't have this book), so now it's just me. I generally have all the same gear, but with a few exceptions. I've replaced the mattress with a comfortable, lightweight cot. It takes up less space and gives me more room to move around. I also have

FIGURE 9.2: Camping in central Nevada.

a few camping tables and a chair inside my tent. I like to be able to work on my computer and have a semblance of home while I'm away.

RV or Van

Living in a RV has its benefits and challenges. One benefit is that you can have all your things where you want them all the time. No packing and unpacking. If you work a season doing sessions the entire time, then the packing tends to get tedious and annoying—especially if you travel with a lot of things.

> When considering purchasing an RV there are a multitude of considerations. Is this going to be your primary residence in and out of the field? How often will you need to move the RV? Will you be staying for long periods of time in towns without RV waste dump stations or power hookups? These may seem like boring questions, but, considering them before making any decisions could save yourself a huge headache.
>
> If there is any advice I can give a field tech thinking of purchasing an RV is make sure you are confident in your mechanical abilities. RVs are typically built for weekend camping or week long excursions. Most will have difficulty withstanding the constant abuse of a permanent or semi permanent residency, not to mention rugged terrain that comes with archaeology work. Be prepared to come home from a long day of survey to a broken water heater, a leaking sink drain, a frozen dump valve, or any infinite number of problems these fiberglass boxes can throw at you. And, if you can't do these things yourself, be prepared for exorbitant repair costs.
>
> This is not meant to discourage anyone. I thoroughly enjoyed my time teching in an RV. However, be prepared for more labor and logistical planning outside of the field. – David Field

Some downsides to traveling with an RV include just finding a place to park it and paying for it. If you stay in an RV park or a campground, you'll end up paying more than you think. Most of these places have hook-ups for water, power, and a place to dump the "gray" water. I'll let you work out what that is. Amenities included with an RV park or campground could include wireless internet, showers, and a small store. Of course, RVs and vans don't come cheap. Even if you manage to find a good deal and buy one, you still have insurance to worry about. In addition, most of those vehicles get less than great gas mileage. Overcome the aforementioned hurtles, and you still have challenges. Want to go to the grocery store? Gotta take the RV. Want to go sightseeing after work? Gotta take the RV.

Unless you have another vehicle, bicycles, or an understanding friend, the RV could be a real pain.

If you have the money, the will, and the determination to make RV life work, then I think it could be very rewarding and could greatly improve your quality of life and your attitude. Ask your grandparents if you can borrow or rent theirs for a season! I would if I could.

Hotel

> My hotel Holy Trinity: microwave, mini-fridge, and internet. Free breakfasts that don't start until 7 am when you have to be in the field by 6:30? That doesn't do me any good! – Jennifer McGuire
>
> If you're in charge of booking the room, always strive for the Holy Trinity—free breakfast, free internet, and mini-fridges. – Bill White

Most of your lodging for archaeology work will be in a hotel room. A lot of the small towns in America do not have hotels that are listed on the popular websites, such as Priceline.com and Hotels.com. A simple Google (or your search engine of choice) search of the town you need and the word "hotel" will usually provide a list of accommodations, some with reviews. When you call, be sure to have at the ready your list of things to ask about. So, what should you ask about?

> I worked for an outfit associated with a major . . . . university and the project manager had no idea how to get a good rate on a motel. Never asked for a group rate or a weekly rate, just accepted whatever price they gave him. – Jennifer McGuire

Before I even get to price, I like to make sure the hotel has the amenities I need. For long-term stays, a microwave and a refrigerator are essential. You can do without a refrigerator if you have a cooler and an ice machine nearby, but that is a hassle in the summer time. You can do without a microwave too but be prepared to bring a hot plate and cooking equipment or something equivalent. In this day and age, having the Internet is important for most people. Ask the receptionist whether the Internet is wireless or ethernet and whether you have to pay for it separately or not. Do they have breakfast? It might save you money if they do. Find out when the breakfast starts before you decide not to bring any breakfast food. Many hotel breakfast start-times are after you have to start work. Some minor things I ask about include the types of beds (two doubles or one larger bed), type of TV

(I can hook my computer to certain types), air conditioning, swimming pool, laundry, and whether they have an exercise room.

There are some things to think about when discussing the cost of the hotel room. Hotels often have a AAA discount. A lot of smaller chains will have corporate discounts for people working in the area, and most have weekly rates. If you get a weekly rate, find out whether their week is five days or seven days. Also, find out what the refund policy is. You may have to leave early for one reason or another and would probably like your money back.

Summary

Whether you choose to live in your car, in a tent, in an RV, or in a hotel room, the choice you make for lodging could make or break your sanity on a strenuous project. Even if it's an easy project, your choice of lodging could be a huge factor. Figure out whether you like to live alone in the wilderness, how important having the Internet is, and how often you want to see friends and coworkers when making your decision.

10 HOTELS

The first hotel I ever stayed in for archaeology was on my second project. The developer had ties to the Marriott chain of hotels, so that's what we stayed in. The Courtyard Marriott that was across the street from the project area was full when I got there, so some of us were assigned to the JW Marriott down the street. That was one of the nicest hotels I've ever stayed in, despite the hurricane damage.

A few months before we got to Miami, a hurricane had blown out many of the windows in most of the buildings in southern Florida. For some reason, the management at the JW Marriott was fixing the windows in the corner rooms last. So, we got those rooms since we weren't paying for them. We still had some windows, just not all of them. The broken ones were boarded up. The rooms were still amazing, though.

In the rooms were massive beds with fancy bedding and pillows, a comfortable chair, and a desk; and the room was a good size. Along the wall, opposite the bed, was a granite-topped credenza with a 40-inch flat screen TV mounted on the wall. It was near the spacious granite countertop. There was even a phone in the bathroom.

Walking back from work, muddy and dressed in field clothes, was interesting. We had to walk through the marble covered lobby and into the golden elevators. I swear that every day the elevator attendant thought we were robbing the place. I felt bad being so dirty and covered in mud, but there wasn't much we could do about it. They moved us to the less-fancy hotel a few weeks later. It was more "our style."

If you have to live in a hotel room, there are some things you can do to make your life easier and more satisfying. In my experience, one of the big reasons people don't stay in cultural resource management (CRM) is because they are lonely, unhappy, and bored. Those are all things that you can control. Let's talk about how to control those factors and increase your quality of life.

Quality of Life

I worked on a project in 2012 that lasted for six months. The motel that was provided us was my home for 10-day sessions, with only four days

Field Archaeologist's Survival Guide: Getting a Job and Working in Cultural Resource Management by Chris Webster pp. 75–80 ©2014 Left Coast Press, Inc. All rights reserved.

FIGURE 10.1: Happiness in a hotel room, for me, is a cold chardonnay after the workday.

off in-between. . . . I brought my own bed linens from home each time I checked in. I also burned some incense to make it feel and smell more like home. If they were putting me up in a room I hadn't stayed in before, I would wipe down nearly every surface with a disinfecting wipe. I'm not too concerned about germs, but it made it feel cleaner and smell fresher in the room, which made it easier for me to relax. – Jennifer McGuire

So, how do you live in a hotel and not be absolutely miserable? The most basic way I can put this is to alter the room so it feels like home (Figure 10.1). Make it your home and think of it that way. When I'm out in the field, I say things like, "When I get home, I'm going to read my book and have some wine". I'm not talking about my permanent home. I'm talking about my hotel room, or my tent, or whatever I'm sleeping in that night. If you are constantly pining for that home you left, or that you don't even have yet, then you are not going to be happy with your current living situation and that attitude will reflect upon your work and your coworkers. No one wants to hear someone complain all day about how much they think their life sucks.

In my experience, there are two factors that cause someone to live a squalid life in a hotel room. Those reasons include trying to save money and a lack of knowledge regarding efficiently and happily living in a hotel room.

If you're forced to double-bunk (which almost universally sucks), do unto others. Try to get to know their personality so you don't make them mad. Be respectful even if you don't like your roommate. – Bill White

Saving Money

I know that across much of the country archaeologists are underpaid and underappreciated. In some places, such as the Great Basin, pay and per diem are much higher than the national average. An entry-level field technician could conceivably take home $36-40k in an eight month field season when salary and per diem are counted together (calculated at $13 per hour, 40 hours per week, and $125 per diem for eight months). That's not too bad. Personal situations aside, there should be enough money available to live comfortably and happily. It's all about personal choices and deciding what's important to you.

> Check for bed bugs . . . Learn to recognize the signs of bed bug infestation and what bed bugs look like. I was in a room for a few days before I realized the itchy bumps on my arms were not mosquito bites . . . gross! I caught it in a tissue and brought it to the front desk. They moved my room and gave me $10 in quarters to wash all my gear at the laundromat. Not fun. – Jennifer McGuire

Make the Room Your Own

Before I ever bring any of my gear into a hotel room, I first clear out all the hotel stuff that I don't need. You know what I'm talking about. I move the binders of information, the coffee maker, the little plastic signs, and anything else I'm not going to use. There is usually space on top of the TV cabinet or on the shelf in the closet for those things. I also put the phone on the floor and unplug and move the alarm clock. You'll likely never use the phone, but don't unplug it just in case the hotel staff, or your crew chief when you don't wake up, needs to call. I haven't used the alarm clock since I got a smart phone. Unplugging it and storing it away frees up one of the few power outlets in the room. I always bring at least one power strip. There will never be a time when you don't need it if you have one. Trust me. New power strips often have a couple USB ports which can be handy for charging phones, cameras, tablets, and many other, USB-powered devices.

> I found that I needed a make-shift mudroom. Mine was always just inside of the door when you walk into the room. – Jamie Palmer

Next, I remove the comforter off the bed. Aside from being germ ridden, I usually don't need it since I am a hot sleeper. If you fold the comforter up and stuff it into some out of the way corner of the room, then the maid staff is unlikely to put it back on when they clean the room. If they continue to put it back on regardless of where you put it, then notify the front desk, and they'll take care of it. Whatever you do, don't throw the comforter on the floor at the foot of the bed. This goes back to living in a small space and quality of life. Also, if your room is clean and organized, the hotel staff is more likely to leave you alone.

Wet Boots? Stick newspapers in them and put them on the heater in your hotel room. They should be dry by morning. Watch out for the smell! – Bill White

Finally, in some hotel rooms where space is a premium, you might need to do some rearranging. If there are two beds and you don't need the other one, you can dismantle it and lean the mattresses up against the wall. This frees up room for gear, a workout, or a crazy dance party. Do what makes you happy! Just be sure that if you move anything, put it back the way you found it before you leave. There is a really good chance that you'll stay at that hotel again sometime, and you don't want to burn any bridges. Also, if you trash the room and your company is paying for it, they may not ask you back for another session. Use your phone or camera to take pictures of the room before you do any major rearranging. If you forget, you can always look in someone else's room.

Double the size of your hotel room . . .

If you're lucky enough to have a single occupancy room on your project (a surprisingly rare "luxury" these days), but are still booked in a room with two beds, you can almost double your living space by flipping the second mattress and box springs up on their sides and placing them against a wall. Often, the bed frame is simply four pieces of particleboard slotted together. Carefully take the frame apart (particle board can break fairly easily) and you now have much more space in your hotel room for things like exercising, rearranging other hotel furniture, or setting up your illicit hot plate or electric grill! Just remember to put things back together before you check out and remember, if you break it, you buy it! – Russell Alleen-Willems

Organization

Organization is the key to a happy life in a hotel room. They are just too small and cramped to have all your stuff laying around. I always sort my clothing into the dresser drawers, and I hang up what I can. These are small things you can do to make it feel like home, albeit temporarily. Anything that doesn't need to be in the room—such as an empty suitcase—can go back in your vehicle. Before I get distracted with work and hanging out with the crew on the first day of the session, I make sure to put everything in its place, and I put away all my bins and things. If you leave it for later, it likely won't get done.

Food

There are three ways to handle food while in the field. The easiest way is eat out at restaurants and fast food places. This isn't the healthiest or cheapest option, but if you do it right, you can have leftovers every other day and not have to eat out every night. The way that requires the most preparation is to cook up a bunch of food before you leave and heat it up when you want using your room's microwave. A vacuum food saver is handy for this task. The food saver bags can be microwaved or boiled to heat the food inside. Finally, you can bring cooking equipment and cook everything you need right in your hotel room (Figure 10.2). Plan out how you're going to handle your food situation a few days before you go into the field. Grocery shopping in your hometown might provide better options than the small town you might be staying in for the session. The next chapter goes into cooking extensively so skip ahead if you're sitting in a hotel room right now and are hungry!

> I know a lot of CRM archaeologists rely on the free continental breakfast as a *per diem* preserver (when it's available) but sometimes the choices can be pretty sparse, especially in terms of healthy foods. Here's what I like to do: take a packet of instant oatmeal, put in your hot water, and then mix in one of those small containers of peanut butter. Pair with a banana, apple, or orange, and you've got a great breakfast!
> – Andrew Sewell

Cooking in a hotel room is a subtle art, and it requires patience. Before you bring a bunch of gear out, however, check to see if your room has a stove or oven. Some do. Also, ask the hotel if they have an outdoor grill for guests to use. They aren't just for meat and vegetables, and you can easily boil water in a pan on the surface. Don't forget about cooking in a microwave. Using the right combination of time and temperature, you can cook pasta, meat, eggs, hot cereal, and a variety of other items. The key is usually lower temperature and longer time. Times and temperatures also vary with the power capabilities of microwaves.

FIGURE 10.2: Organization and cleanliness will keep you happy in a hotel room.

As a coffee snob, I never shovelbum without grinding enough coffee for the foreseeable future, and with it bring my pour-over coffee brewer and cone filters along with my electric hot-pot to boil water. This cheap, small, and lightweight brewing system allows me to brew the coffee I like with purified water while on the road. To me this makes the hotel, tent, or car feel a little more like home . . . and we all know that hotel coffee, especially the types of hotels shovelbums tend to stay in, is a few notches below even gas station coffee. – Brandon McIntosh

Finishing Touches

Anything you can do to make your room feel like home should be done. When you spend up to ten days at a time in one room, it can get a little depressing. My wife and I once spent three months in the same room. On my second project, I spent six months in the same room with a roommate. Making the room your own and keeping it clean is a necessity. If you have them, put out some pictures of loved ones and family. Also, put out any trinkets or small items that remind you of home.

Summary

Living in a hotel room can be fun and adventurous. Remove anything you don't need such as the hotel signage, the phone book, and other items that you won't need. Organize the room to suit your needs. Keep your belongings organized and your room clean. Remember to put the room back the way you found it before you leave. Snap a few pictures on your phone to remember how to put everything back. Plan out how you are going to handle food a few days before you go in the field. You'll be happier in the long run.

Your attitude toward living on the road is what you make of it. If you don't enjoy and embrace it, then you will be unhappy. You have to realize that if you stay a field CRM archaeologist, you are likely going to be in the field for quite some time before you land that desk job. When you do get there, you will likely miss going out into the field. Take this opportunity to see new things and meet new people. Every project can be an adventure. If you keep your blackout curtains closed and your TV on, your view of the world will be as myopic as the view out of the peephole in your hotel room door.

11 COOKING ON THE ROAD

When I first started in cultural resource management (CRM), my food was all frozen microwave meals and things that didn't need to cook at all. It was a very unhealthy way to live and wasn't satisfying. Most of the time I'd end up going out for food or picking up something easy. After a few projects where we had cooking facilities at the places we were staying, I think we got used to the idea of cooking on the road.

During a long excavation in Nevada, when my wife and I were living in a hotel room for a few months, we found ways to make dinner more interesting. We had a large electric skillet that we could cook just about anything in, and we learned that a lot of things can be cooked in the microwave. Many archaeologists bring an assortment of appliances on the road with them, and others utilize the equipment already in the room. I once cooked steak and mashed potatoes in a hotel room using just the skillet and the microwave. It wasn't fantastic, but it wasn't that bad either.

Almost no other topic in this book is as varied and controversial as cooking on the road. There are so many variations that one would have trouble listing all of them. I will describe how my cooking and food preparation have evolved (Figure 11.1) since I started in this business, and I'll discuss how others I've observed have succeeded, and failed, in the past.

I'm sure my first grocery trip, on my first field project where I had to stay in a hotel room, consisted of microwave meals, dried goods, potato chips, and wine. Not the healthiest way to live, but I didn't really know what I was doing. For six months, I didn't prepare a single meal in the hotel room. Everything I had was either a snack or a hot pocket. Seriously. I don't know how I didn't gain 200 pounds. Maybe it was the 20–40 mile bike rides after work most days. Must have been.

Equipment and Technique

Bring food and alcohol from home. – Bill White
I love my hot pot. – Jennifer McGuire

Field Archaeologist's Survival Guide: Getting a Job and Working in Cultural Resource Management by Chris Webster pp. 81–88 ©2014 Left Coast Press, Inc. All rights reserved.

FIGURE 11.1: I never leave home without some sort of coffee making equipment. When I have the space, my espresso machine goes with me.

By the time I'd started my second field project, I'd bought an electric skillet. That changed my life. At one point, even though I overcooked them because I was talking to a friend, I made steaks. My girlfriend and I also had mashed potatoes with that meal. I chopped up the potatoes, put them in a plastic container with water, and microwaved them. It had to be done on low power and in 8–10 minute increments. I kept stopping the microwave to poke at the potatoes and check for softness. When they were done, I drained the water out by placing the lid of the container partially over the edge and pouring it into the sink. Then, I added milk, butter, and sour cream and mashed them with a fork. It wasn't a bad meal, for a hotel room.

NOODLES AND MEAT IN A SKILLET

An easy meal to make in an electric skillet is noodles and meat! There are a lot of variations so be creative with this recipe.

Ingredients:

1 pound of meat (hamburger, ground turkey, chicken, tofu, etc.)

Ramen noodles

Vegetables

Cook the meat in the skillet on medium-high. Drain the meat. Wash the meat in hot water if you want to remove excess grease. Next, pour in the recommended amount of water for the Ramen noodles and then pour in the crushed noodles. You'll want the noodles crushed because the skillet is large and shallow and the noodles need to be fully under water. Bring to a boil, then let simmer. Once most of the water is gone and the noodles are done, pour in the seasoning packet that came with the noodles and some fresh, frozen, or canned vegetables. Cover with a lid and cook until the vegetables are done. If you want to be really unhealthy, but make it very tasty, put some sour cream in the mix when it's done! If you're storing a portion for later, then add the sour cream when you eat it. Serve with the worst beer in town and have a dinner party!

On my second field project, I learned that you could make pasta in a microwave. Smaller pastas, like penne and macaroni, are best because you can fit them in a container small enough for some of those small hotel microwaves. Just put the pasta in the container, fill with water to about one half inch over the pasta, and put it in the microwave on medium heat.

You'll have to adjust the heat so the water doesn't boil over or you'll make a mess. Sometimes the defrost setting is good for that because it turns the heat on and off. It could take up to 15 minutes to cook the pasta, but do it in increments of 5–8 minutes so you can stir it. If you don't, the pasta will stick together. Rinsing the pasta before putting it in the microwave will help it to not stick as much. So will putting a little olive oil in the water.

> The importance of having a microwave and fridge in a motel cannot be understated! – Jennifer McGuire

When staying in hotels I was able to do pretty well with the electric skillet, water boiler, and the microwave in the room. Others I've known bring hot plates, toaster ovens, rice cookers, and crockpots. The key is to bring something that has more than a few uses. For example, you can cook just about anything in a skillet. The one downside is that you often have to cook large portions because of the size. When cooking a soup, or other liquid-based meal, you have to fill up the skillet or the food will burn. Rice cookers are great because you can cook rice in the main compartment and steam-cook chicken, fish, vegetables and other tasty items at the same time in the top basket. Also, they're very easy to clean.

> I found rice cookers to be very versatile, not just useful for rice, but they pull double duty as a hot pot. Have even seen them used to bake bread. Buy non-perishables in bulk. The savings may only be a few percent, but with planning you might find yourself eating better. I always prefer traveling with tupperware bins to living out of a suitcase or duffel. They come in handy for hiding contraband, like rice cookers and such. Some hotels are twitchy about cooking in rooms. – Jim Christensen

Hot plates are an old favorite of many archaeologists, but I've never used one. The primary reason is that I didn't want to carry an assortment of pans with me, and they can be dangerous in cramped environments. Trying to balance a pan on the hot plate on the two square feet of bathroom counter you get in some rooms can be challenging. I'm sure more than a few hotel towels and napkins have been started on fire from a hot plate that was too hot and too close.

The Jet Boil system has become very popular among archaeologists lately. They cost a little bit of money but are very useful. The fuel can on a Jet Boil could very well last the season since they are very efficient. You can boil water, make coffee or tea, and heat up meals in a typical Jet Boil. If you buy the accessory pan set you can expand your cooking options. The

Jet Boil is also great because you can bring it anywhere. Since I got mine, I've been waiting for another cold, winter project, where I can bring it into the field and make coffee or soup at lunch. The entire system fits inside of itself and is very light, which makes it very portable. The $100 dollar price tag is prohibitive to some, but it's worth it. Check out the French press accessory that you can get. I have one and use it every day on camping projects. The CO_2 output is low enough that I use it in my tent too.

A necessity for your cooking kit should include spices and kitchen items. Spices can make or break a meal. Get a few good ones and just carry them with you. Bring a set of silverware and some camping dishes too. I have the Sea to Summit plates, bowls, and cups. They lay flat when not in use and can be used as a cutting board. Don't microwave them, though. They'll bubble up, and you can't fix that. Anything you can bring from home, or buy and keep with you, will improve your quality of life and give you a sense of familiarity where ever you go.

Preparation

As my situation has changed through the years, so have my cooking habits. I now have a home base in Nevada, which has changed how I bring food into the field. It's rare that I'll need to hit the grocery store when we get to the base town, and it's also rare that I'll need to eat out at all during a 10-day rotation.

There are two pieces of equipment that have changed how I bring food into the field: a food dehydrator (Figure 11.2) and a food saver. With these two pieces of food preparation equipment I'm able to bring enough food to last me several weeks and I don't end up spending all of my per diem on restaurants, gas stations, and small-town grocery stores. The dehydrator isn't something you'd really want to travel with because it's big, bulky, and has one purpose. If you have a large vehicle and live on the road, you might make it work, but for most it's not a possibility. What the dehydrator will get you is a great way to store fruit and a way to make jerky, if you are one of the four people in CRM that is not a vegetarian (well, five including me!)

Most archaeologists don't eat enough times throughout the day. We are burning thousands of calories and are eating once at lunch and then not again until dinner which could be five or six hours later. Your body goes into "survival mode" if you go that long

FIGURE 11.2: Dehydrating mangos and apples.

without at least something to keep the metabolism up to speed. Eating fruit can help with your calorie intake. The problem with "wet" fruit is storage. Fruit can take up a lot of room in the hotel room, and, it almost always gets squished and banged up in your field backpack. By dehydrating all your fruit before you leave for the field, you'll be able to take a larger volume, and it won't go bad. Just keep it in a zip-lock bag that you can throw in your field bag as you run out of the room in the morning. If you have a craving for a banana or an apple, check the lobby. Most hotels have some fruit set out for breakfast. Some have fruit set out all day.

Use Pedialite for summer nutrition during hot weather. You'll need less than if you had Gatorade and it provides more nutrition. – Bill White

You can dehydrate almost any fruit. I've done kiwi, strawberries, grapes, apples, mangos, and bananas. Some fruit takes longer than others, but you generally need 12 to 14 hours per batch. The standard dehydrator comes with four trays, but you can order more for bigger batches.

The other piece of gear that's changed my life is the food saver. They go by various names and styles, but food savers suck all the air out of a custom bag and preserves your food for a long time.

Because I have a "base of operations," I'm able to make a bunch of meals prior to going in the field. I split them up into meal-sized portions and suck them down into a food saver bag. There are many advantages to this. First, you can fit more food into a smaller cooler. The bags take up less space than containers and you can recycle them when you're done. Also, the bags won't take in water when the ice in your cooler melts. Another advantage to the food saver bags is that you can cook them a number of ways. You can poke a hole or two in the bag and microwave it. If you have a Jet Boil, or a pan, and are camping, you can save on cleanup by just putting the bag in boiling water and heating up the food that way. You can also just take the food out of the bag and heat it up in a pan, or in the microwave, as well. Either way you look at it, you can't go wrong with a food saver.

After work essentials: beer! and food that hydrates you, like cucumbers, tomatoes, melon, etc. – Jennifer McGuire

A little pro tip that I just discovered is to store ice in a food saver bag. Ice is always a problem in the field. You never seem to have enough of it, and it always melts and becomes useless. I may have found a solution to the ice problem and given you a little more drinking water in the process. All you need is a shallow container and a freezer. My small containers measure about five inches by seven inches by two inches deep. I put filtered

FIGURE 11.3: Homemade soup frozen and sucked down with the food saver.

water in several of them and let them freeze for about 24 hours. Then, after removing the ice from the containers, I suck the blocks down with the food saver. This makes a narrow block that you can put vertically between your food, instead of on the bottom, for more uniform cooling. When the ice melts, snip the edge of the bag and pour it in your drinking reservoir in your backpack. Or, you can refreeze the bag and use it again. The ice technique works on other liquids as well. In order for the food saver to suck down a liquid, it has to be frozen. Otherwise, it will not seal properly. I've done that with homemade soup before (Figure 11.3). It's a great way to bring soup into the field with you, especially if you have a Jet Boil or the use of a microwave.

If you don't have a dehydrator or a food saver, you can still save money and increase your nutritional intake in the field. Assuming you have the ability, premake all of your meals. If you can, freeze some of them so they are still fresh at the end of the session. Remember to keep a few of your dinners unfrozen because you'll want those on the first days of the session. It saves power (you know, for the good of the planet) if the microwave doesn't have to work so hard.

Finally, if you don't have any way to make food ahead of time, you can still save time and money. Just go to the store, and buy premade meals. Whole Foods, Trader Joe's, Costco, and most grocery stores have meals that are cooked and ready to go. I'm not saying this is the healthiest or tastiest option, but it's often better than hot pockets and fast food.

Camping Variations

When on a long-term camping project, your cooking options can be slightly different (Figure 11.4). The biggest variable is what kind of equipment is available, and what do you need to bring? On a camping project some time ago, my company provided a gas grill and water for cooking. During other projects, the company provided nothing, and I had to bring whatever I wanted to use. This section will assume that a wide variety of equipment is available. Tailor your specific needs to the project you are on at the time.

When camping for an extended period, I would usually bring a heaping container of pasta salad or some other cold, cheap, food. Then I would make burritos by wrapping veggies, cheese, a little bit of meat (or chocolate and fruit for dessert!) in a tortilla, wrapping that in foil, and letting it warm by the campfire. – Jennifer McGuire

Most campsites have, at the very least, a campfire. A lot of good food can be cooked over, or inside of, a fire. The key is making sure the fire is well developed and that there are some really good coals burning at its base.

For cooking oven-style food, you'll need aluminum foil. Make sure you wrap what you're cooking in at least three layers of standard foil, or one or two layers of the heavy duty foil. The heavy-duty stuff is more expensive, but results in less burned food. When you cook food in the coals of the fire, it's generally a bad idea to put the food in direct contact with coals. They're too hot and will cause the food to cook unevenly. Use a shovel (just about every work camping trip will have at least one shovel available, even in the West) to lift up some of the coals while another person tosses the foil-wrapped food under the coals and into the ash just below the coals.

The cooking time for food under the coals of the campfire will vary depending on the temperature of the coals and the food you're cooking. Potatoes will take at least 40 minutes, depending on the size of the potato. Corn on the cob can take just 10–15 minutes if the fire is hot enough. You can also cook fish, beef, and chicken this way. Make sure the meat gets hot enough on the inside, though. You don't want to get sick with no facilities around. Get creative with your cooking. A potato wrapped in foil with carrots, peppers, garlic, and butter can all cook together and be very tasty!

Most campfires won't have a grill across the top of the fire, unless you're staying at an actual campground. You might have to go back to your childhood and find a good stick to cook with. I've cooked a steak on a stick.

FIGURE 11.4: Cooking tent at a central Nevada field camp.

FIGURE 11.5: Trowel spatula.

It was one strong stick, I assure you. Try to find a branch from a leafy tree. They have less pitch in them than trees with needles. If you have to use a "needle-" type tree, then make sure you hold the end in the fire for a while to burn out all the pitch. You're meat doesn't need to be seasoned with pine tree scent!

To properly grill, either on the campfire or on a camp stove, you need grilling tools. Or do you? Someone may bring a spatula and some long tongs, but most likely no one will be prepared. Fear not! You probably have a spatula in your field pack (Figure 11.5). That's right: a trowel. Even better, a square trowel. Be sure to clean your trowel before you use it for flipping meat. You can also use a shovel for manipulating food in the fire. In addition to using the shovel to lift up coals for roasting, you can use a shovel to place and remove food from a campfire grill, if you're lucky enough to have a grill. Clean the shovel well, sterilize it in the fire, and you can use it to cook on too. Just place the shovel in the fire, and prop it up like a flat cooking surface. You can cook meat right on it. Make sure it's a steel shovel. They handle the heat better. Also, watch the handle! Don't get it too close to the fire, and make sure the conductive heat in the shovel head doesn't get the handle hot enough to start on fire. For extra cleanliness, wrap the end of the shovel in a fresh piece of aluminum foil.

Summary

To be truly happy while living on the road, you need to have your food sorted out. There's nothing like coming in from the field and having a tasty, home-cooked meal. So what if it was home-cooked seven days ago, and you had to microwave it? Whatever it is, it's better than fast food and likely a lot more healthy. Find your style. Cook what makes you happy. Put some thought, time, and effort into your meals. However long your session is, plan out every single meal and make sure you have what you need. If you're in a town or city, you'll likely go out to dinner with the crew at least once so plan for that too. You don't want to bring too much because it might go to waste.

For me, one of the most important things I can do to keep myself sane, happy, and content in the field is to have familiar and tasty foods at the ready. In fact, it might be the number one thing I do to customize my experiences in the field.

12 CAMPING

In an ongoing effort to save money, my wife and I decided to camp for a 10-day session in late autumn, near Winnemucca, Nevada. Our options included an RV park in town and a city recreation area just outside of town. We decided to check out the city recreation area. The drive included a steady climb for several miles that took us into the steep-sided, Water Canyon. It was mid-afternoon, and the entire canyon was shaded. The camping sites were spread out along a small creek that flowed out of the mountain to the south.

We chose the last campsite to minimize traffic to our site. We'd be leaving most of our possessions there during the day and didn't want anything to get stolen. The site was nestled among tall Aspens and sat right next to the creek. It was quite idyllic. What I didn't realize was exactly how high the road climbed to get to the campsite.

The evenings proved quite cold at the southern end of Water Canyon. One morning we awoke to several inches of snow. Our tent was big enough that we were able to prop the air bed up against the wall and bring in our reclining camping chairs. Evenings were spent in a sleeping bag in the chair watching movies on our laptop with the propane tent heater between us. I won't even begin to mention how cold it was trying to use the solar shower by the creek, surrounded by snow.

For some, camping can be way more complicated than living in a hotel room. Essentially, you have to bring your entire room with you. The initial cost can be expensive and your vehicle can quickly fill up with things you thought you just had to have. This chapter will help you go from novice camper to comfortable camper. First, though, let's talk about the different kinds of camping you can do.

Types of Camping

Camping doesn't have to be just in a tent. There are at least five types of camping that I've seen various people do throughout my career. They include truck camping, car camping, tent camping, camping in an RV, and pop-up trailers.

Field Archaeologist's Survival Guide: Getting a Job and Working in Cultural Resource Management by Chris Webster pp. 89–94 ©2014 Left Coast Press, Inc. All rights reserved.

RV Camping

I've only known one couple to use an RV for work. They lasted about a season with it before both of them got out of archaeology and pursued other careers. I don't think the RV was the catalyst for their hasty departure from the field, but it probably didn't help. Refer back to chapter 9 for some tips on RV camping.

Truck Campers

Truck campers are the type that sit on the bed of a pick-up truck. Essentially, these have all the features of an RV, except they are a lot smaller. There are many differences beyond size, though. For example, you won't need an extra vehicle with a truck camper. Just take the truck wherever you need to go. A truck camper can be parked at an RV park, a campground, a hotel parking lot, on Bureau of Land Management (BLM) land, or wherever you want! Many of them still need to have the water tanks filled and the gray water emptied, though. Also, if you don't have strong batteries and solar panels on the roof, you'll need power occasionally.

The biggest cost of a truck camper is usually the truck. A good-sized camper top is going to need a big truck. A new truck will cost upward of $45,000. You can always buy an older truck, of course. Just make sure that the camper top you buy, and the truck you have, will work together. There are variations with each, and not all of the combinations fit.

Pop-Up Trailers

These might be the hidden gem of the cultural resource management (CRM) world. They are light, come in a variety of sizes, don't cost very much, and have a lot of features available. That being said, I've only seen one in use on a project during my career thus far. That might be because you usually need a truck or sport utility vehicle (SUV) to tow one. It can be done with the right car, but you wouldn't want to make the trailer too heavy.

The standard pop-up trailer is square when it is folded up for travel. When it's cranked up, there are often sides that come out for added space. Basically, it's a pop-up tent. Keep that in mind when it's really cold outside. Unless you have a heater, it's not going to provide much warmth. The "deluxe" model trailer can be very large, indeed. I've seen ones that have a queen-sized bed at either end with a table and seating area in the middle, which also folded down into a bed. Most trailers have propane hookups with water and electricity too. The water and electricity might just be outside hook ups, so you'd have to find a campground with those available to use them. For the money, you can't really go wrong with one of these, as long as you have the vehicle to tow it.

Car Camping

In many books on camping, and in department store displays, car camping refers to a camp ground that you can drive to. Your tent and all your supplies are only a few feet away. The car is your base of operations, and is also your storage. In this context, however, I'm literally talking about sleeping in your car. I've known more than a few shovelbums that resorted to sleeping in their cars for parts, or all, of projects. There are many reasons for this. Usually it's because they ran out of money. Some people, though, just want to stay out on BLM land and are fine sleeping in the car or in a sleeping bag on the ground outside. To each her own, I say.

There's not much more I can say about this except that you'd better keep an organized vehicle if you want to sleep in it. Having the ability to put the seat down is crucial. Make sure it's the passenger seat so you don't have to deal with the steering wheel. Also, bring a pillow. There's nothing worse than doing eight miles of survey after waking up with pain in your neck and back. If you do it right, car camping can save you a lot of money in a very short period of time. I wouldn't recommend doing it for the entire season, though, unless you had a van or something suitably large.

I'll mention one variation that a friend has that I thought was particularly clever and could be an option if you want to put in a little work. His vehicle is a Toyota Tacoma with canopy over the bed. In the bed, he built a raised, plywood, platform. The platform sits about as high as the wheel wells and it has trap doors to access storage underneath. The canopy is tall enough that he can put a mattress down on the plywood and sleep very comfortably. Of course, heat is still an issue, but at the right time of the year, this can be a great option!

Tent Camping

Most people in CRM will camp for a project at least once in their lives. The only exception is possibly with those that live in the Southeast. It's just too hot for camping! Well, that's my opinion, anyway. For the rest of us, camping is a great way to save money on those high per diem projects. There are ways to make your camping experience comfortable and rewarding and ways to make it really suck.

On our first camping project in the Great Basin, my wife and I arrived early to set up our mobile palace. Before I get to that, though, I want to describe some of the other tents we saw there. More than a few of the crew, some of whom had been camping for many months on that project already, had small, one- to three-person tents. They couldn't stand up in any of them, and in some they couldn't even kneel without hitting the ceiling. Most of the tents also had a small footprint as well. I saw one, inhabited by a medium-build guy, that was so small that his sleeping bag took up the entire floor of the tent!

The simple fact that most people in the world live in a house, apartment, or somewhere they call home and store their stuff, says that we like that sort of lifestyle. So, what makes someone think they'd be happy staying in a tent where they had to lie down to put their pants on? In the hot, dusty, environments of much of the West, they also have dirt and rocks to consider. To clean the tent, everything has to be removed. That's probably not much of an issue since most tents are so small, but it's still an inconvenience.

Now, I'll tell you the two ways I've camped. One way was with my wife, and the other way is with just me, after my wife left archaeology. When we first started camping, my wife and I had a small, borrowed tent. I quickly realized that if I wanted to spend months at a time in the same tent, I'd want to be comfortable. After we started working in the West we bought an REI Hobitat 6. The best feature of the tent was that it had practically vertical walls which meant I could fully stand up across most of the footprint. For bedding, we started with sleeping pads and sleeping bags. After rolling off the sleeping pad one too many times, we bought a queen-sized air bed. We were able to fill the bed by plugging an extension cord into our SUV. That changed everything. A good night's sleep is worth more than gold on projects where you have to work really hard during the day.

We also had some wire shelves that could be put together in a number of configurations. They were handy for storing clothing, food, and toiletries. On the top of the shelves, we put our laptop and external hard drive. In the evening we would sometimes prop the airbed up against the wall of the tent. Then, we'd bring in our reclining camping chairs and watch movies on the laptop. It was very comfortable, and we went to bed content every night.

Now that I'm camping by myself, but still have a large tent, I've changed the layout a bit (Figures 12.1–12.6). The tent is now an REI Kingdome 6. It's more rectangular than the Hobitat, and the walls aren't as vertical, but it's still got a ton of room. The tent has two flaps that come down in the center and can be a room divider. I put one side down and put a fold-up cot in the back half. One of the Action Packer tubs I use for gear becomes my nightstand, and the back half of the tent is transformed into a small bedroom. In the front half, I have clothes on hangers hanging from parachute cord, a table, a lamp, my field gear, and a chair. It's nice to be able to work on the computer inside the tent and out of the wind and weather. I'm even able to make my coffee in my Jet Boil in the morning on my table. The tent is big enough that short-term cooking won't produce enough CO_2 to cause a problem. It's the little things, really.

On the front of the tent I have the vestibule that is part of the rain fly. This is where I store the cooler full of food and usually my work boots. If you're in an area with bears, though, you need a bear-proof cooler. Don't store food in your car because they'd can get in there too. Any wet gear goes in the vestibule too. It can dry under the vestibule and not get my tent wet and muddy. I also have a rubber floor mat that keeps most of the dirt and dust from coming in the tent. When dirt does get in the tent I have a dust pan and small broom to get it all back out.

This probably sounds like a lot of gear to some people, and don't get me wrong, it is. However, aside from the cot, my chair, and the table, it all folds up and gets put away into two Action Packer tubs. Actually, I can fit everything I just mentioned, and more, in my Prius. Add one cot, a chair,

and some extra clothes, and you've got my wife and I on a camping trip. That still all fits in a Prius. Now, since space isn't a problem for the efficient packer, you just have to worry about cost.

Much of this stuff can be bought at a variety of venues. As archaeologists, we're hard on equipment. No tent maker expects a tent to be used for 100 days in the hot sun! They just aren't made for that. The same goes for a lot of our equipment. It's not made for the duration and abuse we inflict on it. So, buy your equipment new at a store that will take it back if it breaks.

The best, although not the cheapest, for return policies, again, is REI. They have a return policy that is simply made

FIGURE 12.1 (top): Tent entrance with floor mat and cooler outside.
FIGURE 12.2 (middle): Work clothes hanging inside tent near center partition.
FIGURE 12.3 (bottom): Worktable and chair. Water containers sitting on Action Packer tub with clothes inside.

FIGURE 12.4 (top): Cot with Action Packer nightstand, sleeping bag, and pillow.
FIGURE 12.5 (middle): Bedroom setup.
FIGURE 12.6 (bottom): View of "living room" from "bedroom."

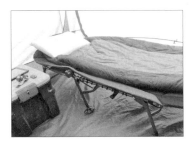

for archaeologists. I wouldn't recommend this myself, but if you wanted to get a new pack, pair of boots, and a tent every season they'd let you. Well, to a certain point. I've heard you can get banned from returns if you abuse it. So I wouldn't try. What I would do is try out a tent for a session to see if you like it. Sometimes you just have to live in something for a little while before you know if it's going to work out. Assuming you didn't destroy it during that time, you can return it and try something else. The same goes for much of what they sell.

Summary

We covered a lot over the course of this chapter. Don't feel like you have to do exactly what I've outlined here. I'm willing to bet that I'm the only one that sets up my tent like I'm on an African expedition in 1905. However, many field archaeologists do at least a combination of what I've discussed, and many have still other styles of living that are just as good. The point is that you need to do whatever you can to keep yourself happy. Consider every avenue, and try different things. You may not realize it, but it's the little things that will keep you happy and coming back for more.

SECTION 3

LOCATION, LOCATION, LOCATION

The ability to know where you are at all times is incredibly important in archaeology. You have to know how to use a compass, how to use a Global Positioning System (GPS), how to read a topographic map, and how to recreate a map of your surroundings. Whether you're a cultural resource management (CRM) archaeologist or an academic archaeologist, mapping and determining your location is a skill that all archaeologists must have.

This section starts with the basics: the Universal Transverse Mercator (UTM) grid (chapter 13). You have to know where you are before you can know where you are going. The Township and Range system (chapter 14) is used across much of the US and is covered in this section. Many states identify sites by a common system known as the Smithsonian Trinomial site number. The history of the Smithsonian system and how it is used is covered in chapter 15. Finally, the ability to hand-draw a map of a site is a skill that is rapidly being lost. Knowing how to draw a map of a site on paper will help you when you need to draw a site map with a GPS. Hand-mapping is covered in chapter 16.

13 THE UTM GRID[1]

I went several years in cultural resource management (CRM) before I really knew what theUniversal Transverse Mercator (UTM grid was and how it came about. No one told me, of course. I had to figure it out myself. My first excavation project was laid out on a one-meter grid that had a starting point based on a UTM coordinate. I didn't understand where the numbers for the units were coming from because I didn't un-derstand the grid system. Since the project was so short I never really had a chance to find out why it was the way it was.

By the time I started working in the West, I had a firm grasp as to how the grid worked and how to use it. I saw people fumble through it, though, because they didn't understand what direction to move in to make the numbers increase and decrease. Don't make that mistake! Learn why things work and how they work, so you can teach others!

Many people have heard of coordinates on the earth related in latitude and longitude. Frequently, the borders of states and countries are defined by a segment of a line of latitude or longitude. Much of the border between the US and Canada lies along a latitude line called the 49th parallel. In archaeology; however, we like to do things using the metric system, when we can, and the UTM grid is the preferred way to identify the locations of everything from sites to individual artifacts.

What is the UTM?

The UTM grid divides the Earth into sixty vertical zones that are each six degrees of longitude wide and are centered over a longitude line. The zones are numbered 1 to 60 with zone 1 starting at 180°W longitude; zone numbering increases to the east. North America is covered by zones 10 through 19. The zones are separated into 20 latitude bands lettered from "C" to "X" (south to north) with "I" and "O" omitted (more on that later). Each zone is 1,000,000 meters wide, and the 500,000 m mark is located in the center. If you are walking in a UTM zone, the northing will increase as you walk north and the easting will increase as you walk east. The northing is your distance, in meters, from the equator and the easting is unique to

Field Archaeologist's Survival Guide: Getting a Job and Working in Cultural Resource Manage-ment by Chris Webster pp. 96–98 ©2014 Left Coast Press, Inc. All rights reserved.

the zone. That's the quick and dirty description of the UTM grid. Now for the details.

Details and History

Can you guess who designed the UTM grid? That's right, the military. It was designed by the Army Corps of Engineers in the 1940s to better calculate distance between two points. Calculating distance between points on a latitude-longitude grid required complicated trigonometric formulas (Remember, a calculator was the size of a house back then!). The UTM grid required only the Pythagorean theorem ($a^2+b^2=c^2$) to calculate distance, which can be done on a piece of scratch paper. I've done it many times to calculate distance when I didn't have a Global Positioning System (GPS) unit in front of me.

The Mercator Projection

"Mercator" in UTM refers to the Mercator projection of the Earth developed in the sixteenth century. It was designed to represent the earth on a two-dimensional piece of paper while preserving angles and approximate shapes, but it distorts distance and area. The transverse Mercator is similar but uses non-linear scaling to preserve distance and area.

As I stated above, the grid is divided into sixty zones, which are each divided into twenty sections or "latitude bands." The bands run from 80°S to 84°N. The first band is labeled "C" in the south, and the last band is labeled "X" in the north. The letters "I" and "O" are omitted because the military always eliminates them due to their similarity to the numbers "1" and "0." Most of the bands are eight degrees high with band "X" extended to 12 degrees to cover all of the land on the earth. The remaining letters, "A," "B," "Y," and "Z" are also used. They cover the western and eastern sides of the Antarctic and the Arctic regions, respectively.

Location Using UTMs

A typical coordinate in the UTM system needs to have four parts. They are the zone, band, easting, and northing. A coordinate in Nevada, for example, could read "11S 260909mE 4339066mN." That translates to zone 11, band S, with an easting of 260909 and a northing of 4339066. The easting indicates that the coordinate is in the western half of grid zone 11S. The northing translates to 4,339,066 meters north of the equator. If you are in the southern hemisphere, the northing still refers to a distance to the equator. The grid was designed so that you never have a negative number because negative numbers can't be used to calculate distance.

CHAPTER 13

We typically walk on a particular northing or easting when we are on a pedestrian survey. Whenever I'm walking an easting line (maintaining a constant northing) I like to think about the fact that I am walking parallel to the equator. It's a little amazing that this system is set up that way and that I can parallel a line that is over four million meters away. Geometry is fun!

Excavation Coordinates

On many excavations, a local grid is set up for locating artifacts. Often, the grid will have a center point, or datum, of 100/100 or 1000/1000. Although, I have seen datums set at 0/0 and far off the site, in a corner, so every coordinate has a northing and an easting (as opposed to a southing and a westing, which no one really uses. Negative northings and eastings are used, though), or any combination of just two cardinal directions. With the near ubiquitous use of survey equipment, such as the total station, some companies are just using UTM coordinates for excavations. That is my preference, since, often the local grid is converted to UTMs after the excavation is complete.

Summary

The essential elements that you need to know in order to position yourself on the earth using the UTM Grid are the zone, band, easting, and northing. With these four pieces of information you can locate your position down to the centimeter, with the right equipment. There is a lot more information on map projections, datums, and the UTM grid online. Take a minute to learn more about the tools that we use every day. It will make us all better scientists.

Notes

1 Paul A. Longley, Michael F. Goodchild, David J. Maguire, and David W. Rhind, *Geographic Information Systems and Science*. 2nd ed. (West Sussex, England: John Wiley and Sons, 2005).
2 Gregory G White and Thomas F. King, *The Archaeology Survey Manual* (Walnut Creek, CA: Left Coast Press, 2007).

14 TOWNSHIP & RANGE[1]

Until I was told to figure out the "quarter sections" for a number of sites, I really didn't know what the Township and Range system was, or how to use it. We even worked on a project in Utah where we were assigned entire sections to survey, and I didn't know what those sections were based on. It seems silly thinking back on it now, but I should have asked. I'm willing to bet that others I worked with didn't understand the system either.

I didn't have to worry about township and range until I came to the West, so I never learned how it worked. At various times, I'd seen people using funny looking square rulers, and I still didn't ask questions. We all have a tendency to not ask questions because we don't want to look like we don't know what we're doing. Some people in this field can be very judgmental, and we all know that. So, we stay quiet and fumble through. After you read this chapter, go to work, and lay down some knowledge on your crew.

Archaeologists on the West coast, in many of the Plains and central states, Alaska, and Hawaii are likely familiar with the Township and Range system. In the Great Basin—where I work—and in surrounding states, the "legal location" of a project area or an individual site is given in quarter-quarter sections using the Township and Range system. But, what is the system, and where do we get coordinates like "T17N, R15E, Mount Diablo Meridian?" We are about to find out. Let's start with a short history of the rectangular survey system, also known as the Public Lands Survey System (PLSS).

History of the PLSS

The PLSS was originally proposed by Thomas Jefferson. It began after the Revolutionary War ended and the federal government became responsible for massive areas of land west of the original thirteen colonies. The government wanted to distribute land to Revolutionary War soldiers in reward for service, and they wanted to sell land as a way to raise money. Before this could happen, the land needed to be surveyed. Two laws helped create the PLSS as we know it today (until 1973, that is). The *Land Ordinance of*

Field Archaeologist's Survival Guide: Getting a Job and Working in Cultural Resource Management by Chris Webster pp. 99–101 ©2014 Left Coast Press, Inc. All rights reserved.

CHAPTER 14

1785 provided for the systematic survey and marking of public lands. In 1787, the *Northwest Ordinance* established a rectangular survey system to give coordinates to the land parcels. The PLSS has been in continuous use since 1785 and is the basis for most land transfers and ownership today. The current procedures for accomplishing the PLSS were set down in the *Manual of Instructions for the Survey of the Public Lands of the United States* in 1973.

Not all land was included in the survey. Lands not surveyed included beds of navigable bodies of water, national installations (military, parks, etc.), and land grants already in private ownership. According to the Bureau of Land Management's (BLM) website, almost 1.5 billion acres have been surveyed for the PLSS to date (2013). The BLM is the record keeper for over 200 years of survey information, which often includes the original surveyor's notes and hand-drawn maps.

Now that we know how it started, let's talk about exactly what the PLSS is and how we get to township and range coordinates.

How is the PLSS Used?

As stated above, the PLSS is used to divide public land. Since the system was started after the Revolutionary War, it mostly only applies to new land that was acquired after that time. That's why none of the thirteen original states were included—there was little public land left.

The PLSS divides land into six-mile square townships. The townships are then divided into thirty-six sections. The sections can then be divided into half, quarter, and quarter-quarter sections. It may not make sense that the quarter-quarter sections aren't $1/16$ sections, but, once you write it out and use the system it works. The sections are numbered starting in the northeastern corner and move left/west. The numbers snake down going back to the right/east (7 through 12) in the second row then back the other direction and so on. The section numbers end at thirty-six in the southeastern corner. Each section is usually 640 acres, or a one-mile by one-mile square. The one-mile squares make it easy to do block surveys in the West.

The township and range coordinates are based on regional meridians and baselines—37 of them. Range is designated east and west of the principle meridian for the region, and township is designated north and south of the baseline. When reporting the location of a parcel of land using township and range, it's necessary to include the principle meridian. For much of California and all of Nevada, the principle meridian runs through Mt. Diablo in California. So, a proper land designation for somewhere in

Nevada would be, "Nevada, Mt. Diablo Meridian, Township 21N, Range 15E, Section 35."

Regions, Principle Meridians, and Baselines

There are several areas of the country where the township and range system is different for various reasons. In Ohio and Indiana—where the surveys started—the townships are six-miles square. The surveys are named, but the names are not named based on the principle meridians; and, the numbering system and starting points are different. In Louisiana, things really get crazy. They are based on parcels of land known as *arpent sections,* and they predate the public surveys. An arpent measures 192 feet, and a square arpent, confusingly called an arpent, is about 0.84 acres. The parcels are designed to give settlers living on waterways beachfront property and tillable, farmable land. So, they are oddly shaped. French arpents were 2 to 4 arpents wide and 40 to 60 arpents deep. Spanish arpents were 6 to 8 arpents wide and 40 arpents deep. Section numbers frequently exceed 36. If you plan to work in Louisiana, find out how it all works from your company, or your crew chief, before going in the field. You'll be smarter and happier for it.

Summary

Now you should be an expert on the PLSS. When someone says the site is located in the SE ¼ of the NE ¼ of T17N, R15E of the Mt. Diablo Meridian, you'll know what that means. I'll admit that I was out in the West for quite a while before I really knew what the Township and Range system really meant. I could certainly find my way around the system, but I didn't know what it was based on. Find out where your principle meridian originates from and impress your friends.

Notes

1 GeoCommunicator, *The Public Land Survey System* (PLSS), http://www. geocommunicator.gov/GeoComm/Isis_home/home/Isis-plss-description .html, 2013, accessed July 29, 2013; National Atlas. 2013 *The Public Land Survey System* (PLSS), http://nationalatlas. gov/articles/boundaries/a_plss .html, accessed July 29, 2013; Gregory G White and Thomas F. King, *The Archaeological Survey Manual* (Walnut Creek, CA: Left Coast Press, 2007).

15 SMITHSONIAN TRINOMIALS[1]

The first site I worked on with a site number that I was aware of was 8MD1. I didn't realize the significance of that site number until I learned about the Smithsonian Trinomial system. For a group of people, archaeologists, that are obsessed with history, it's pretty cool knowing that you're working on the first site to have been either identified, or at least given a site number, in that county. It's also pretty daunting to know that you're working on the 15,000th site identified in a county.

It always amazes me when people rattle off site numbers for a project, and they have no idea where they came from. Whenever I get the chance, I explain the site number to people, and most are surprised at how much information you can get from one.

Many states use a standard convention for numbering archaeological sites. When I first saw one of these site numbers, it looked like an indecipherable string of numbers, but with an underlying structure that I just couldn't make out. There is a good chance that you've either already been exposed to these numbers, or that you will be soon. These are called "Smithsonian Trinomials" and they look something like this:

26WA12477   9PM201   23AR9236   8MD1
50TX3546   12TN30   32GNA3476

Breaking down the Trinomial.

The word "trinomial" means "three parts." You may remember learning about binomials in math–don't put the book down! I won't mention math again. The first number represents the state. The state numbers run from one to fifty. The District of Columbia, American Samoa, the Federated States of Micronesia, Guam, the Marshall Islands, the Northern Mariana Islands, Palau, Puerto Rico, and the Virgin Islands do not get a number (who knew we had so many territories?). The numbers mostly run in alphabetical order. The exceptions are Alaska (49) and Hawai'i (50). They weren't states when the system was devised.

The letters are a two-digit code (sometimes three) for the county. On site records and site reports these letters are sometimes capitalized, and,

---

Field Archaeologist's Survival Guide: Getting a Job and Working in Cultural Resource Management by Chris Webster pp. 102–104 ©2014 Left Coast Press, Inc. All rights reserved.

sometimes only the first letter is capitalized. There doesn't seem to be a consistent practice of using either one.

Finally, the third part of the trinomial is the site number, sort of. The entire trinomial is actually the site number. The number at the end of the trinomial represents the number of the site in succession with the rest of the sites that have been reported in that county. For example, a site number of "9PM201" means that site was the 201st site in Putnam County (PM), Georgia (9) to be given a site number.

History and Development

The Smithsonian Trinomial number was devised and perfected over a number of years by the Smithsonian's River Basin Survey (RBS). The RBS operated in a number of states and needed a comprehensive system of designating new sites. The RBS started in 1946, and by the end of fiscal year 1947 in the Missouri Basin, 376 sites in seven states had been recorded. Paul Cooper, an RBS staff member, was instrumental in devising the first incarnations of the system between 1946 and 1947. The early system was based on an even earlier system that was used in Nebraska during the 1930s for Works Progress Administration (WPA) projects. Other states were using a system similar to Nebraska for WPA fieldwork, but none were identical. Carl Miller, also an RBS staff member, added county codes for several southeastern states in 1958. He was following some state universities and historical societies that had already incorporated the county code.

Although the RBS program ended in 1967, individual State Historic Preservation Officers continued to assign site numbers based on the Smithsonian Trinomial System. Now, many states issue site numbers using that system. A lot of spatial data can be determined just by being able to decode the Smithsonian Trinomial. Think about it. Without knowing anything about a site you can narrow its location down to the county level in a matter of seconds.

Other Systems

California

The system in California is similar to the Smithsonian Trinomial in that it is a trinomial and incorporates the county and a sequential site number. Instead of the two digit state number, however, California uses "CA". Also, they use a three-character county code instead of a primarily two-character convention. Otherwise, the entire trinomial looks much like the Smithsonian version.

CHAPTER 15

New Mexico

New Mexico uses the University of New Mexico's Laboratory of Anthropology system. Some agencies, however, still use the Smithsonian system. Find out what system the project you are on is using.

Summary

The Smithsonian Trinomial system is one that most archaeologists have used to number sites across the country. It has a long history and will likely continue to be used for a long time to come.[2]

Notes

1 Rose Chou, *Smithsonian Trinomial Numbers* (Electronic document on file at the National Anthropological Archives, Smithsonian Institution, Washington, DC, n.d.).
2 Rose Chou, Personal Communication (National Anthropological Archives, Smithsonian Institution, Washington, DC, June 2012).

16 MAPPING

We arrived on a prehistoric site after a long walk through the hot and dusty northern Nevada high desert and immediately started to look for, and pin, artifacts. The site was covered in deep sand that had formed into low hummocks by thousands of years of fiercely blowing winds and snow-melt. As we systematically walked over the site, the crew chief, also the project's principal investigator, was not just looking for artifacts but was looking at the depositional and erosional processes that created the landscape features within the site. He was also observing bunches of sage-brush, small juniper trees, and other vegetation, carefully noting their locations, size, and where they were in relation to artifacts and features.

When we finished marking all of the artifacts, concentrations, features, and site boundaries, the principal investigator pulled out a small table on a telescoping monopod. On it he placed a piece of graph paper and set himself up near the center of the small site. For the next thirty minutes he swiveled around the table while sketching in big features and artifacts. For finer detail, he walked to objects he wanted to sketch onto the map, noting the distance and bearing from his location.

When he was finished, the principal investigator had created one of the most detailed, and well-illustrated, sketch maps I'd ever seen in cultural resource management (CRM) archaeology. At first I thought it was too busy. After looking at it for a minute, though, I realized how accurate it really was. You could get a sense of how the site was laid out just by looking at the sketch map. It's possible to do that with other, more simple, sketch maps but not to this level of detail.

There is a subtle art to mapping that takes a little creativity, intuition, and practice. Most companies I've worked for, at least in the last three or four years, just used a sub-meter Global Positioning System (GPS) unit to map sites. A hand-drawn map is often created for features, but a GPS is still used for site maps. One problem I've seen with some people's GPS maps is that they lack a lot of important information. Sure, all of the features, artifacts, and major roads are on there, but, they lack the finer details that help characterize a site. It's my opinion, based upon experience, that it's difficult to know what to put on a GPS map unless you've had experience

Field Archaeologist's Survival Guide: Getting a Job and Working in Cultural Resource Management by Chris Webster pp. 105–110 ©2014 Left Coast Press, Inc. All rights reserved.

with pace-and-compass maps. I'm not sure why that is, but I think it has to do with the more personal nature of a pace-and-compass map, as opposed to a GPS map. The things I like to see on a site map, aside from the artifacts, features, and site boundary include major landforms, drainages, creeks, roads, old trees, some vegetation, rock outcrops, and any other prominent features. The skills required to recognize what is important for the map, and what is not, seem to come from learning how to draw a pace-and-compass map.

Pace and Compass Maps

Defining Your Pace.

The first thing you need to know is what the length of your pace is. Your pace is something you probably already know from doing surveys. For those of you that don't, here is how you do it. First, find a straight stretch of uninterrupted ground like a road or parking lot. Next, roll out 30 meters from a roll-up tape measure. Now, simply walk at a normal speed, without stretching out your stride, and count the number of steps it takes to get to the end. You might want to do this several times so you can take an average. This number is your pace. I'm about 6'1" tall, and my pace is about 43 steps. I have freakishly short legs. I know some tall people that have a pace under 30 steps! Still, some people like to shorten or lengthen their stride to make it exactly 30 steps. I would say that you should do whatever you are comfortable with, as long as you are relatively accurate and consistent.

Map Supplies

Now that you have your pace, it's time to get your map supplies together. Pace-and-compass maps are relatively low tech, which is why they are easy to do (Figures 16.1 and 16.2). To gather the data for your map, you will need a note-

FIGURE 16.1 (top): Notebook, compass, and pencil.
FIGURE 16.2 (bottom): Two pencils—a 0.5 mm-led mechanical for fine detail and a 0.9 mm-lead mechanical for boundaries and think lines—and a ruler with 180-degrees markings.

book (or smartphone for you tech savvy people), a pencil, and a compass. That's it. I told you it was low tech.

Deciding What's Important

The first thing you have to realize is that not every site is going to be mapped the same way. For example, if you have a large lithic scatter with no tools and no features, you may just want to accurately map the boundary, a few flakes and natural features, and that's it. On the other hand, if you have a mining site with prospect pits, shafts, refuse piles, and other features, you may want to first map the features then simply draw the boundary around them. Basically, you have to figure out what your boundary is being created by. It might be that your boundary is being created by a project APE (area of potential effect), pipeline corridor, or some other artificial boundary.

Taking Measurements

There are a number of ways to take site measurements. I'll cover two of the most popular types. This first method assumes you have a site boundary marked out in the field. Start by picking a point near the center of the site, usually the datum (the datum isn't always in the exact center of the site and may be represented by a large boulder or tree). Depending upon what state you're working in, there may or may not be a physical datum on the site. If the datum will be determined in the company office using a Geographical Information System, then just pick a natural feature, such as a large rock or a tree, or, simply put a group of pin flags in the ground where you plan to start. Once you have your starting point, it's time to take your first measurement.

If you have clearly defined boundaries, then it's usually easier to record your first boundary measurement going north. On your notepad you can start by writing "datum" (or tree, pin flags, or whatever) on the top line (Figure 16.3). Using your compass—set to the proper declination—find north, and pace to the boundary. After you've paced to the boundary, write down the distance and bearing to your point from the datum on

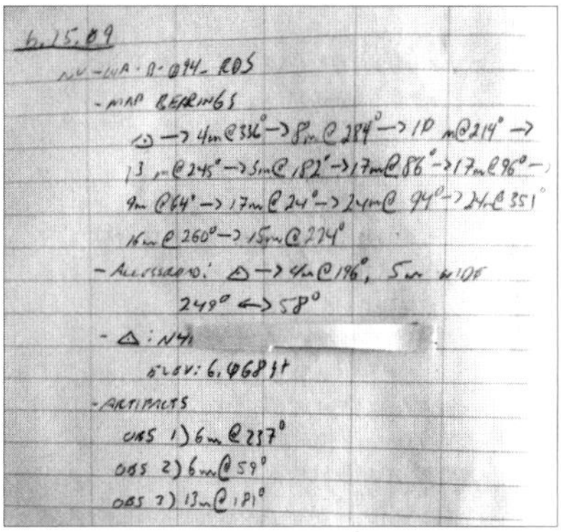

FIGURE16.3: After walking around the site, you should have a table of distances and bearings that define your site boundary.

the next line in your notebook. It will look like this: "12@0°". That translates to, "walk twelve paces in a direction of north from the datum." For my next boundary point, I usually walk counterclockwise, so sight in your next point and walk to it. The next point can be anything you want, but you want to be able to draw a nice, curved, line around the site. Some corners will require multiple points. For small corners, I'll take points at the start of the corner, the apex of the corner, and the end of the corner. Once you have your point's distance and bearing, write it in your notebook. It might look like this: "15@275°". Make your way around the entire site and back to that first point you took north of the datum. That's the boundary! Next, you'll want to take points on all the numbered artifacts, features, and whatever else your crew chief wants you to. On small, manageable sites—50-m × 50-m or so—take all of the artifact and feature points as a distance and bearing measurement from the datum. On larger sites, you may have to just do whatever makes sense. Be flexible!

You can also map a site without a field-defined boundary. A case where this is advantageous would be where the site consists solely of features. Mapping a site using features or numbered artifacts can be done a number of different ways. If you don't have many features or artifacts, you can simply take distance and bearing measurements from the datum for every point. Once you draw in the features and artifacts, you can draw a line around the site. There are other ways to do it too. You just have to decide what makes sense for that site.

Sketching out the Site.

Once you have all of your measurements, it's time to sketch them out on graph paper (Figure 16.4). Before you start, though, make sure you check and see whether your company has a list of map symbols they'd like you to use. Check with the crew chief and find out. You want to be consistent with the other crews and the rest of the company. When you are ready to start sketching, you'll find that one of the most difficult decisions to make is where to put the datum and what scale to use so that the entire site fits on the map. It can be a bit frustrating, but, you'll learn over time how to do it with fewer mistakes. You'll need some special skills for putting

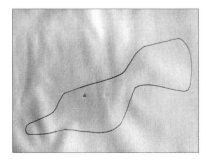

FIGURE 16.4: The initial site boundary sketch from the measurements in the notebook.

the points on the map too. You might also want a clear protractor or a round, 360-degree, translucent scale with a straight ruler attached to the center point. I have an engineering scale that I use for distance. Keep in mind that the squares on the graph paper are not going to work for scaling your drawing. The scale will be determined by whatever method you choose and whatever fits best. I find which scale on my six-sided engineering scale works best for the site and then draw my scale on the page to fit that measurement.

Put the points on the map in the order that you took them. Draw the datum point first. Then, measure the number of paces that match your scale to the north and draw a point. Next, find the next bearing and measure the appropriate distance. When all the boundary points are done, draw in your boundary. Next, graphically draw in your features and artifacts. By graphically, I mean draw the center point and then illustrate the feature around it (WARNING: you may need to learn to draw what you see around you!). Once the cultural items are on the map, sketch in the landforms, prominent vegetation (i.e., trees and other significant natural features), rock outcrops, streambeds, and whatever else makes sense. If there are a lot of features and artifacts on your map, then just freehand the vegetation and geological features relative to the site (Figure 16.5).

The last items to sketch, and sometimes the most difficult, are the topographic lines. Some people have a difficult time representing hills, ridges, and drainages topographically. This just takes practice. Look at a topo map while you are out in the field. Understand what you are seeing on the map,

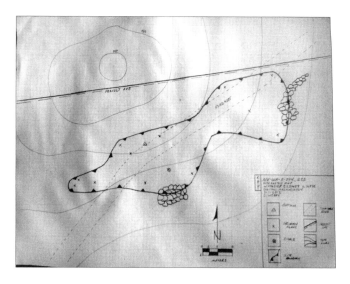

FIGURE 16.5: Completed site sketch.

FIGURE 16.6: An example of a map legend.

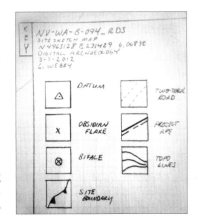

and apply it to the landscape around you. Sometimes, while out on survey, I try to visualize drainages, mountains, and ridges as though they had topo lines on them. Try it sometime.

Finishing Touches

The level of detail in the finishing touches on your map will likely be determined by how anxious your crew chief is to get out of there and on to the next site. At a minimum you will need a north arrow, a scale, a data block, and a legend (Figure 16.6). The north arrow, for some people, is like a signature. I've seen all kinds of variations. Some people like to design fancy ones and some use just a generic arrow. Make it your own. The scale is based on the scale of your map. Again, I've seen everything from fancy and detailed, to generic. Do what you think best fits the site and your company's preferences. The data block contains all the site information. At a minimum it usually contains the site number, the date, the company name, the words "site sketch map" or something equivalent, the datum coordinates, and your name. The legend should contain every symbol that's on the map. If you put it on the map then put it in the legend.

Summary

Drawing a sketch map is a skill that every archaeologist should develop. The intricate details of a site are easier to see when you've had to draw them by hand. Eventually, no one will draw paper maps anymore. As tablet computers become more advanced, and more field ready, you will likely be drawing sketch maps on them. It'll feel like a combination between GPS and sketch maps. Personally, I'm looking forward to it!

SECTION 4

GOOD TO KNOW

This section of the book could contain hundreds of chapters. Regionally, there are many things you should know in order to go from being an OK field archaeologist to a great one. Maybe there is a unique pottery type that is only slightly different from a common one, and you know the difference. Maybe certain depressions are actually 100-year-old root cellars, and you can only know that based on the historical resources available for the area. In archaeology, especially cultural resource management archaeology, because you can literally work anywhere in the country, you are always learning something. If you don't learn at least one new thing on every project, then you aren't paying attention.

17 DIMENSIONAL LUMBER[1]

Surveying in a mining-heavy area in Nevada is very challenging, and you have to be on your toes when it comes to historic artifacts. On one particular project in central Nevada, we recorded several hundred mining features per crew, per day. The majority of the features were small depressions in the ground called prospect pits and stacks of rocks called cairns. Many of the features had no artifacts associated with them, so we had to rely on other sources to date them. Those other sources included historical documents that told us when the mining began in that area and when it was at its peak. Another source was the wooden posts that were sometimes included with the stacks of rocks. If most of us had known more about the reason for the sizes of those posts, we could have avoided recording some of the more recent ones.

In the West, we commonly come upon historic sites, usually mining related, that have wooden posts in various locations. Like everything else in archaeology, we measure them. What do those measurements tell us? Do we measure them because, as archaeologists, we obsessively measure everything? Yes. And no. The measurements can tell us something.

History

What is "dimensional lumber?" Basically, it's lumber that has been dried, planned, and cut to a specific width and depth, as measured in inches. Common sizes found on sites are 2 × 4 and 4 × 4. Large 6 × 6 and 8 × 8 beams can be found as well. The common sizes, referred to as the "nominal" size, are based on the wood's green, or rough, dimensions. The finished size is actually smaller than the nominal size.

History

Prior to the late 1800s, building lumber was usually processed close to where it was produced. As markets grew, and lumber was needed further and further away from mills, it became apparent that standard sizes would be needed. After 1870, some sawmills began to plane wood with machines to make rough lumber more uniform. The boards were usually only sur-

Field Archaeologist's Survival Guide: Getting a Job and Working in Cultural Resource Management by Chris Webster pp. 112–114 ©2014 Left Coast Press, Inc. All rights reserved.

faced on one side, known as *S1S*, and sometimes on two sides, *S2S*. As late as the 1920s, some mills based their pricing structure on rough, saw-sized dimensions. The reduced actual sizes of the dimensioned boards also meant a reduction in weight, which resulted in a reduction in shipping costs.

The early 1900s brought regional sizing standards to the market. In 1902, the *Pacific Coast Lumber Manufacturers Association's Standard Dimensions and Grading Rules for Export Trade* determined that boards under four inches in thickness, or six inches or less in width, could be worked an eighth of an inch less for each side of the edge surfaced. In 1906, certain board sizes in North Carolina could be dressed by as much as an eighth of an inch. By 1919, after shortages associated with World War I, it was clear that national standards should be adopted. The 1919 meeting of the American Lumber Congress (yeah, that's a real thing) determined that standards needed to be written for lumber sizes.

National standardization of lumber sizes began in 1921. Several major lumber barons approached the Secretary of Commerce, Herbert Hoover, and proposed a standardization of lumber size and grading standards, and, requested that the standards be published by the Bureau of Standards. The first national standards didn't come until after many more meetings and revisions. The date was November 6, 1923. Of course, there were problems, and the actual establishment of the standards didn't take place until July 23, 1924.

Over the next few decades battles over how much a board could be dressed were fought, won, and lost. Lumber barons across the country all had their own agendas. Much of the controversy centered around money, of course. Suppliers that used the Panama Canal to ship lumber wanted smaller boards because shipping costs were determined by volume, not weight. Interstate shippers were concerned more with shipping boards dry rather than wet, or rough, since shipping cost in those cases were based on weight. Finally, in 1961, with subsequent revisions until 1963, the lumber standards we have today were pretty much set.

Measuring Lumber

Of course, you have to start by addressing the quality of the artifacts you're measuring. When you are measuring lumber and looking for a certain measurement, it's important to recognize whether the wood is heavily weathered or not. In dry environments, wood tends to crack and separate. In the West, snow and rain can get in wood, freeze, and cause the wood to split. The measurement is virtually useless in a lot of those cases. You can sometimes still find a useful place to measure though. Look at the ends.

CHAPTER 17

Sometimes they haven't split yet. Or maybe just one end hasn't split yet. Don't give up. There's often a way.

Once you find an un-warped piece of lumber to measure it's time to apply the lumber standards. From the figures above, it's clear that if you measure a 4 × 4 post, and it measures to anything larger than 3½ inches on a side, then the post is likely older than 1961. The closer the post measures to its nominal size the older it probably is. Of course, as with everything historic, you can't rely on one artifact to date your site, and you need to cross-date with other artifacts.

Summary

Lumber sizes throughout the early twentieth century varied depending upon region and place of manufacture. Starting in the 1920s, the sizes of milled lumber started to get smaller than the nominal size. By 1961, lumber sizes were a size that is similar today. When you measure lumber now, the further the measurement is from the nominal size, generally, the older it is. On archaeological sites, especially in arid regions, lumber is often the only thing left. If it's intact, not warped, then it can be measured. Getting an accurate date for the site could mean the difference between recording the site and not recording the site. More importantly, it could mean the difference between being eligible for listing on the National Register of Historic Places or just another site.

Notes

1 L. W. Smith and L. W. Wood, *History of Yard Lumber Size Standards* (Madison, WI: Forest Products Laboratory, Forest Service, U.S. Department of Agriculture 1964); *The Engineering Toolbox*, "Softwood Lumber Sizes," http://www.engineeringtoolbox.com/softwood-lumber-dimensions-d_1452.html, accessed August 21, 2013.

18 MUNSELL BOOK OF COLOR[1]

My field school was actually an Earthwatch Expedition that took place in Olduvai Gorge, Tanzania. Olduvai became famous when the Leakey family began finding H. erectus and H. habilis fossils in the mid-twentieth century. For the field school, we were digging in deposits that dated back nearly two million years.

At some point during the excavation, we had to map part of the trench that we had already excavated. When the mapping was finished, I helped the crew leader determine the Munsell colors of the different strata. I had to admit that I'd never seen a Munsell book before, and I didn't know what to do. Of course I found out that it's a fairly simple tool to use as long as you're consistent. My African friends were surprised that I, a recent undergraduate in anthropology, didn't know what the Munsell book was and what it was used for.

Many people have used the Munsell book, but few know of its origins and where the numbers we assign to colors come from. Read this chapter and go out and amaze your friends and coworkers with your new and amazing knowledge!

If there is one standard in archaeology across the country it is the *Munsell Book of Color*, usually shortened to just Munsell. My first experience with the *Munsell Book of Color* was on a dig in Olduvai Gorge, Tanzania, Africa, during my field school. The field director asked me to Munsell a profile—yes, it can be used as a verb—and I had no idea what he was talking about. He then told me that it was a British thing. They always Munsell soil samples and profiles. I later learned that it is not, of course, just a British thing.

Whether you are a field rookie or a seasoned veteran, there is likely something you can take away from this chapter. Honestly, I never really did understood what the different pages really meant and what value and the chroma are. Maybe you learn that in art class, but I haven't had an art class since second grade.

Field Archaeologist's Survival Guide: Getting a Job and Working in Cultural Resource Management by Chris Webster pp. 115–118 ©2014 Left Coast Press, Inc. All rights reserved.

Origins of the Munsell Color System

The idea of using a three-dimensional shape to represent all possible colors was first explored in the mid-1700s. Several shapes were chosen including a triangular pyramid, a sphere, a hemisphere, a cone, and a tilted cube. The most sophisticated design was a slanted double cone conceived of by August Kirschmann in 1895. Kirschmann's color solid was the first to recognize the difference between bright colors of different hues. All these models encountered problems when trying to accommodate all possible colors and none were based on the measurement of human vision.

Albert Munsell, a professor of art at the Massachusetts Normal Art School, wanted a way to describe color that would use decimal notation instead of color names which could be misleading. He started on his new system in 1898 and finished it seven years later with the publication of *A Color Notation* in 1905. The first *Munsell Book of Color* was published in 1929 and improved on deficiencies regarding the physical representation of the theoretical system. Experiments performed by the Optical Society of America in the 1940s resulted in improvements to the system and the familiar notations that we know today. The Munsell system we now have is used, not only for archaeology, but for skin and hair colors in forensic pathology, matching soil colors for the United States Geological Survey, shades for dental restorations, and in some breweries for matching beer colors.

What is the Munsell Color System?

The Munsell color system specifies colors based on three dimensions: hue, value, and chroma. For non-art majors, I'll explain what these are. Hue is defined as "the degree to which a stimulus can be described from colors that are described as red, green, blue, and yellow." Other definitions state that hue is a "pure" color without tint or shade. In the Munsell system, there are five principle hues: red, yellow, green, blue, and purple. There are five intermediate hues for a total of ten hues which are then broken up into ten more hues each for a total of one hundred hues. Those hues are given values.

The next metric, value, refers to the lightness of a color. In the Munsell system, it is measured vertically from a value of "0" (black) to "10" (white). The colors from black to white, including the various shades of gray in-between, are called neutral colors. All other colors are called chromatic colors. We'll see why below.

The third metric, chroma, is measured from the center of the color system, horizontally, and represents a color's purity. A lower chroma is washed out, such as in pastels, and a higher chroma is brighter. There isn't necessarily an upper limit for chroma. Some hues have a higher potential chroma than others. For example, light yellow colors have a higher potential chroma than light purples do because of the nature of the human eye and the physics of color stimuli. Normal reflective materials have a chroma into the low twenties, while some fluorescent materials have chroma values as high as thirty.

So what does this all mean for archaeology? Well, most of it doesn't mean a whole lot. We use a very small wedge on the Munsell Hue Wheel. Sometimes it's good to know the details about the things we use every day.

Getting Your Own Munsell Book

Want your very own *Munsell Book of Color?* The full book, with over 1,600 color chips (in glossy or matte) costs nearly $1,000. You've probably never seen the full book. I never have. That's because they sell a soil version. *The Munsell Washable Soil Color Charts* (2009 Edition) runs for about $185. You can find it at Forestry Suppliers online, or just search for it. The Munsell Store also sells a pack with just the 7.5YR and the 10YR page for $75.

Alternatives to the Munsell Book of Color

There are no accepted alternatives to the *Munsell Book of Color*. Don't despair, though, technology is changing and may provide an alternative. There is an iPhone application that claims to have all the colors in the book for $4.99. There is a lot of skepticism regarding this app, however. The primary complaint lies with the variability of screens and brightness. For example, if you have a screen protector on your device, it might slightly change the color representation. Also, if the brightness isn't set the same way on all devices that are using the application, then the same person could read one soil sample a number of different ways. It's an intriguing idea, though, and I'm looking forward to not carrying the book around.

Summary

Everyone needs to know how to use the *Munsell Book of Color*, or Munsell. Understanding the three metrics of hue, value, and chroma that make up the color chart is important to understanding the science behind the color.

Notes

1 *Adobe Technical Guides*, "The Munsell Color System," http://dba.med. sc.edu/price/irf/Adobe_tg/models/munsell.html, accessed April 14, 2013. Albert Henry Munsell, *A Color Notation* (Boston, Massachusetts: G. H. Ellis Company ,1905). *Munsell Color*, "About Munsell Color," http://munsell. com/about-munsell-color/, accessed April 12, 2013.

SECTION 5

THE END, FOR NOW

All good things come to an end. For cultural resource management (CRM) archaeologists, the end comes every year around November. For some, the end comes, and they never come back. This section covers topics related to not doing CRM archaeology any more. Hopefully, by this time you've read enough of the book to be able to keep yourself happy for a long time in CRM. But unfortunately, sometimes there just aren't any jobs, and you have to do something else. Read this section, pay your bills, and get back in the saddle. This can be a rewarding career if you do it right. And yes, there are right ways and wrong ways to do CRM archaeology.

19 UNEMPLOYMENT

We'd just returned from the field after an eight-day session in central Nevada doing survey on a property owned by a mine. While I was in the field, I posted photographs of projectile points and interesting features to my Twitter and Instagram accounts. At some point, I'd mentioned that I was on a particular mine. I didn't know that the first rule of the mine was that you don't talk about the mine.

Within fifteen minutes of arriving back at the office, the principal investigator on the project fired me for tweeting the name of the mine. I couldn't believe it. Luckily, she said they were not going to record my dismissal as a firing but as being laid off. Since it was October in the Great Basin, and work was winding down, the chances of finding another position were vanishingly small. That's when I decided to file for unemployment.

As a cultural resource management (CRM) archaeologist, you will often find yourself without work. There may be a lull between jobs, or you might be off for three to five months for the winter. In this business, you never know what the future, let alone the next month, will bring. Of course, the smart field tech will save enough money in order to plan for unforeseen events, such as unemployment, but nobody's perfect, and hindsight is 20/20. So, even if you're morally or politically opposed to unemployment, it's good to know about it and how to get it, just in case.

Filing for Unemployment

I've always been a bit too lazy to file for unemployment in the past. I figured that working in several different states throughout the year would just make it way too complicated. Also, the unemployment procedures are different for every state. This chapter will discuss filing for and collecting unemployment in the state of Nevada only; however, it's similar for other states.

The first thing you should do if you want to collect unemployment benefits is to use your favorite search engine and look for "unemployment" in the state you are a resident of. The Nevada system is quite simple and after

Field Archaeologist's Survival Guide: Getting a Job and Working in Cultural Resource Management by Chris Webster pp. 120–123 ©2014 Left Coast Press, Inc. All rights reserved.

searching "unemployment in Nevada" I found it right away. In Nevada there is an online filing system that will ask you questions to assess whether you can even file online, or if you have to use the phone system. The question that stopped me when I did it was whether I had worked solely in the state of Nevada for the past 18 months. That is the period they use to assess how much you will qualify for. I decided to test the system, because I had one two-week job in Georgia at the beginning of the 18-month period, but the rest of my work was in Nevada. I thought that I could just forget that part. That was my first mistake.

When I filed in Nevada, I answered the test questions satisfactorily and the website directed me to the online filing system. Then, I answered a bunch of questions and finally made it down to my work history. That's when I backed out of my plan to forget about the little Georgia job. Once I admitted that I'd worked in Georgia, the system immediately kicked me out and told me to use the phone filing system. The government knows everything. Don't try to fool them.

The phone system is automated and asks the same questions as the online system. It never even asked me about the Georgia job because this is when you find out that they are only looking about nine months back. After that, it took about fifteen minutes to complete the filing process by phone. At that point I thought I was done. The automated system told me that my claim would be evaluated and that I'd be contacted.

The next day I received a call from a person at the unemployment division. He asked me almost all of the same questions, including the names and addresses of my last employers (during the last 9–12 months). He was able to instantly pull my financial data from those employers and determine that I had made about $33K during the last four quarters. That qualified me for the maximum (in 2011) unemployment benefit of $396 a week for a maximum of 26 weeks (or $10,296). I was told that there might be federal taxes assessed on this "income" (Nevada doesn't have a state tax), and I was given the option to hold 10% of the disbursement each week. I elected to do that because I didn't need the headache of dealing with pulling taxes out of savings in April. My research has shown that many states don't take taxes out of unemployment checks and that you'll have to do it yourself come tax time. Find out what your state does so you're not surprised in April.

Once You're in the System

In many states, including Nevada, you have to file each week to get your check the following week, or later that week. You also have to keep a log of the jobs you apply for. They say you should apply to at least three to four jobs each week but it is almost impossible to enforce. Especially if you have a career that doesn't have many open positions (such as archaeology in the winter). You can be asked to show your job log at any time. Here in Nevada, you have to satisfy the unemployment division when they ask to see your job log or they could demand back all the money they gave you up to that point.

For Veterans

Since I'm a veteran, I had an additional complication in Nevada. Veterans are supposed to go to Nevada Job Connect to see if they can be assisted in the job search. All governments like to treat veterans differently which is sometimes good, but, sometimes it's just a hassle. My representative was a good guy and didn't give me too much trouble.

Consequences of Unemployment, or, Benefits?

If Nevada Job Connect had been able to find me a job, regardless of the conditions of the job, I would have been required to take it. If you are offered an interview, you have to take it. If you don't do these things, they can submit your case for adjudication, and you could lose your benefits and all the money they've paid thus far. In Nevada, as in other states, you have to file once a week. You can file starting at 12:01 am on Saturday night here. The sooner you file, the sooner they pay you. I filed online at about 9 am on Sunday morning and by Wednesday the money was in my account. If I waited until late on Sunday then I was paid on Thursday.

The way they pay you in Nevada is by putting the money into a Wells Fargo savings account, which is accessible with a very restricted debit card. You get charged for too many withdrawals, too many balance inquiries, for trying to take out money that isn't there, and for calling customer service. You can avoid fees by going into the bank, so there's that at least. When I was on unemployment, I would just go to the Wells Fargo ATM, withdraw the money, and since I banked with Wells Fargo, I put it right back into my account. You can elect to have paper checks sent, but for most people, there is too much of a lag between filing and receiving the check. Also, it's the twenty-first century. Who gets paper checks?

Summary

Even though you may not want to collect unemployment, it's there in case you need it. You may have to file in several different states for maximum benefit, which will almost be a full time job in itself. Many people have political objections to filing for unemployment and think that too many people feel entitled to it and end up just staying on it as long as they can. I feel that CRM archaeology is one of the few professions where people earn their unemployment every year. We work hard during the year, and if there simply isn't any work over the winter then you should be able to draw unemployment. Consider it a gift from the people of the state you live in for helping to record and preserve their history.

20 PREPARING FOR THE WINTER

For my first four years in cultural resource management (CRM) archaeology, I managed to find work that kept me busy through most of the winter. There were a few times where I was unemployed for a few weeks at a time, but for the most part, I was working. To do that, you sometimes have to keep moving.

As my wife and I were planning to take a vacation to Europe for the winter, we saw a job on Shovelbums advertising an excavation up in Washington State. There was no per diem, but it was close to my parent's house, so we could just stay with them. It was going to be a unique project excavating a very old prehistoric site, so we decided to try for it and put off the vacation.

We got the job and left the diminishing field season in Nevada to work in one of the coldest and snowiest winters on record in Washington. I'm glad we did, though. It allowed time to reconnect with my parents, for good or bad, and we met friends that we still talk to today. One of them is even on the CRM Archaeology Podcast with me. Consider your options and try not to miss good opportunities when they come by.

Preparing for the winter is not a subject with which every archaeologist can relate to (Figure 20.1). In many parts of the country, you can simply work all year long. If much of the work is based on construction projects, though, there is still a slowing down of activity for some reason, which means you'll be out of a job. For the parts of the country where winter shuts down archaeology completely, this chapter is mostly for you. Anyone can take advantage of the tips and advice in this chapter, though, if they want to save money and be prepared.

Save That Per Diem!

The enigma of per diem—it can be so much money if you play it right. I'll start with an example. When my wife was still a shovelbum, we were on all projects together. Sometimes the per diem was great, and sometimes it wasn't there at all. However, sharing lodging, a vehicle, and equipment has its advantages. One big advantage is the ability to bank a ton of per diem.

Field Archaeologist's Survival Guide: Getting a Job and Working in Cultural Resource Management by Chris Webster pp. 124–128 ©2014 Left Coast Press, Inc. All rights reserved.

FIGURE 20.1: Winter archaeology.

My wife and I spent the several months before I went to graduate school on a big, long-term project in northern Nevada. The per diem rate was $109. We were each getting about $16 an hour in pay. Since the project was behind schedule, and the total cost of the development was somewhere north of $3 billion, the client had authorized unlimited overtime. So, most of us never took a day off. Our principal investigator was great, though, and would let us take a day off whenever we wanted, just to recharge our batteries. If you wanted to take four days off you could do that too. We chose to work most of the time, since I wouldn't be working in graduate school. Over the course of the next couple months we stayed in our tent at a motel/RV park. The cost was $7 per night. In just two months, we managed to save close to $10,000 and put a bunch of money on our credit cards. That money was what kept me fed during graduate school. That, and the fact that my wife was still in Nevada sending me per diem checks!

Even though per diem can be really good, many people still don't manage to save any money by the end of the season. I'm not sure why that is. All I can tell you are ways to try to save money. We've already discussed a few in previous chapters. You can buy good gear that won't break, or at least has a great return policy. Cooking your own food in the field or before you leave for the field can save money. Sharing a room with a friend can also save money. A quick note about sharing rooms: I'm not an advocate of companies requiring people to share rooms. However, if two people choose to share a room, that's different.

Savings Accounts and Investments

Ideally, you can live off your pay checks and put all the per diem in the bank. That's if you're camping for free. Otherwise you pay for the hotel then put the money in the bank. Now, I'm not a banker, and I'm not providing investment or banking advice, just good ideas that you can try. Deciding what to do with the money once you put it in the bank is a tricky situation.

Since you never know when you might be out of work for a few weeks, or months, it might be a good idea to keep a few thousand dollars in a savings account that is attached to a checking account. Many credit unions even have interest bearing savings accounts. Make sure they don't have withdrawal limits or minimum balance requirements. You may have to take all of it out at once to fix the transmission in your '81 Bronco. I keep most of my savings in a higher interest online savings account with no minimum balance and no withdrawal penalties or limits. The bank used to be called ING Direct but they were bought by Capital One and are now Capital One 360. Nothing seems to have changed with the accounts, though. With that account, you do need to have another checking account to use to transfer into and out of the online account. There are other ways to get money into and out of Capital One 360, but that is the simplest.

Save enough money so that you can live for three or four months in the winter. That figure is going to be different for everyone and depends on your bills and the lifestyle you want to live. We'll get to that later.

Once you've got your savings fortified, you can think about investments. Safe investments are individual retirement accounts (IRAs). You can put a certain amount of money into them each year, up to a maximum amount. There are usually fees, penalties, and/or taxes to be paid for early withdrawals, so, watch out for that. IRAs are intended to be retirement accounts so don't put in anything you might need anytime soon. Build that up and you can talk to a broker about other investments, or just do it yourself. Either way, make sure the savings is built up before making investment decisions.

Resist Temptation

I'll be the first to tell you that you should live your life and be happy. Saving all your money every single day and not spending any on yourself and then dying of a horrible disease in your thirties is not the way to go. I've seen it happen. That being said, you should also not go around throwing money at bars, cars, and toys. (I'm speaking mostly to the guys here.) Many women I know have an easier time of saving money and not buying frivolous things. Not all of them, of course, but some.

If you need a vehicle to get you from project to project then that should, of course, be a priority. If you need camping gear for your next great project, then get it. Just don't buy anything crazy that you don't need before you get your winter savings taken care of. Even better, wait until you've put away some money in your IRAs too. By taking the right projects and working in the right areas, you can save a bunch of money and have the things you want. You just need to budget. Oh, and I'm aware that many people on the East coast have no idea what I'm talking about. The per diem is just too low across much of the area and often only covers your hotel and maybe your food.

Winter Work

For some, this is the type of job where you can definitely take a few months off in the winter. Some people travel, some work on other projects like writing and catching up on reading, and some just don't want to work as hard as they did over the summer for twelve months a year. Either way, you have to figure out what you're going to do over the winter, and, the sooner you do the less stress you'll have.

For those that want to work through the winter, there are several options. If you want to keep doing fieldwork, but you live in a region that gets too much snow, then you might have to start looking elsewhere. There are plenty of areas where work is available all year long. Keep in mind, the market will be saturated with field techs looking for jobs in these areas. Also, many regions are very selective when it comes to the people they give work too. Either you have to know someone, get lucky, or work your way closer and closer to that region. The Southwest and the Great Basin are like that.

Another winter work option is to find a lab position. Keep your ears open for those massive excavation projects going on over the summer, even if you never work on them. When it comes time to start looking for winter work it wouldn't hurt to contact those companies and see if they have a need for extra help in the lab. Working in the lab provides its own set of problems. There is usually no per diem available, and you'll have to either get an apartment or find someone to room with. A temporary lab position isn't the best option for everyone but can be a rewarding learning experience if you can make it work.

Planning to NOT Work

If you can manage it, I personally think it's best to not work. I'm not saying you should lay around and eat cookies the entire time. Learn something.

Do something. Go somewhere. We have been given the gift of a dream job, and many people just don't realize that. Right now, you might be sweaty, dirty, and reading this in a seedy hotel room with no money in the bank and an empty refrigerator, but this really is a dream job.

Where else can you travel around the country, work outside in the wilderness, and get paid to do it? Sure, those jobs are out there, but those people don't get to be archaeologists. Once, on the Miami job I've mentioned elsewhere, I was with a friend, and we were walking across the street to the parking lot, and the excavation we were working on, to get my car. As I was working the combination lock on the gate, a middle-aged man in a tuxedo with a stunning woman on his arm, stopped on the sidewalk and asked us what was going on inside the fence. We told him what we could about the excavation and what we were doing. He told us that he thought our jobs were really great and that he always wanted to be an archaeologist. He also mentioned that he watched us all the time from his condo. I asked where it was and he pointed to the top floor of a massive high rise across the street. He owned the penthouse condo, which was worth several million dollars easy, and yet he still wished he could be doing what we were doing. If only he'd known I was only getting $11 an hour. That's the power, and the draw, of this field, though. So, take advantage of it.

If you can take a few months off in the winter because you saved money during the field season, then do it! Spend that time writing a book, traveling to the places others only read about, or writing a blog that describes your experiences in archaeology. Take the time off that you very much deserve, but use that time wisely. Don't throw away the gift of time because you can never get it back. I know that sounds ominous. It's supposed to. Don't be one of those people that did 20 years as a field tech and have nothing but a lot of parties, a sore back, and calloused hands to show for it.

Summary

Preparing for winter takes time and planning if you want to have fun and achieve your goals. Once you figure out what you want to do, be it work, travel, writing, or climbing a mountain, work to achieve that goal. Don't wait until November to make plans. Don't even wait until July to make plans. Figure out your goals, and make them happen as soon as you can. Even if you can only put away $10 every week in the spring, you'll still be working toward your goal.

When you're sitting in a coffee shop at 10am on a Tuesday in January reading a book and someone asks you what you do, tell them you're an archaeologist and that you're living the dream!

21 COMING BACK

I've never left archaeology, so I don't have any personal experience related to coming back. There have been others I know that did come back, though, because archaeology just has a draw that some of us can't resist.

By writing this book, I hope to help keep people from leaving the field of cultural resource management (CRM) archaeology. Still, for a variety of reasons, people do leave. Almost no one, however, got into this field because of any reason other than a passion for history. It's that passion that draws us in—in the first place—and it's that passion that keeps us here. If we had to leave, it's that passion that brings us back.

Using Your Network

Even if you were only in archaeology for one season, you probably know more people than you think you know. When you're ready to come back, contacting these people should be the first thing you do. If it's been a while, some of them might even be in a position to give you a job. It never hurts to ask. Before you call or send an email to that long lost contact, get your information in order and do a little research.

Update Your Résumé or CV

A gap in employment is not really an oddity on a shovelbum's curriculum vitae (CV). If it's been a while, though, you might want to touch it up a bit. With every job, you've likely learned, or used, a skill that could benefit you in CRM. Have you talked to clients? Did you use any common computer programs? Were you a supervisor in any way? Look at all the responsibilities you had in your non-archaeology jobs and highlight those on your CV. Don't waste time talking about how you were responsible for cleaning out the deep fryer at McDonald's. Talk about how you dealt with high pressure situations and a fast-paced work environment. I know archaeology is only rarely "fast paced" but it still sounds impressive to a potential employer. Maybe you continued to read about archaeology in your region or read some interesting papers. Those things may not belong on the CV, but they are certainly worth mentioning in an interview. It shows that you weren't totally out of touch and that you retained an interest and a familiarity with the field. William "Bill" White's eBook called *Résumé-Writing for Archaeologists* is a great resource for making a great résumé.

Update Your Social Media

Many employers will Google potential employees before they come in for an interview. Google yourself and see what comes up so there aren't any surprises. Another service you should update, or sign up for, is LinkedIn. I mentioned this earlier in the book, but I'm mentioning it again because that's how important it's becoming. Once you get your profile updated, find the company you're applying to and follow them. Try to connect with any employees that are on there too. When you do connect, find out what groups they are a part of by looking at their profiles and then join those groups. Participate in discussions on those groups if you can. The more an employer sees you interacting, the more they will see that you are interested. Keep your name in front of them. When you post in a group, the other group members get an email about it, with your name in the header. That helps get your name on their radar without directly contacting them.

If you have other social media accounts, verify that your privacy settings are set properly. You might not want some posts to be public and searchable by Google. Again, Google yourself a couple times, and see what comes up.

Starting Over

If you've exhausted your network, and still can't find work, then it's time to start over, or go back to school and get a Master's Degree. If you're starting over, then I'd suggest you read Bill White's book *Résumé-Writing for Archaeologists,* and go back to chapter one of this book. Between these two resources, you should be able to find something.

Good luck and welcome back!

APPENDIX A: CVS AND RÉSUMÉS

Curriculum Vitae (CV) and résumés are discussed in chapter 2. What follows are examples of a CV and a résumé.

Christopher James Webster

1600 Pennsylvania Avenue, Washington, D.C.   *chriswebster@digtech-llc.com; 425.293.3925*

EDUCATION

University of Georgia, Athens
      Master of Science: Archaeological Resource Management
           Completed July 31, 2010
      Thesis: "Archaeological Investigations at 9PM201, Putnam County, Georgia"
      Studies included:
- Preservation Law
- Geographical Information Systems
- Geophysical Techniques
- Geomorphology
- Archaeological Theory
- Prehistoric lithic and ceramic analysis

University of North Dakota, Grand Forks
      Bachelor of Arts: Anthropology
           Completed May 2005
      Studies included:
- Physical Anthropology
- Aviation
- Mathematics
- Photography

Work Experience (Months)

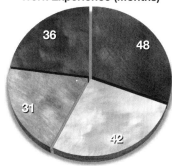

■ Crew Member
▧ Archaeology Crew Chief
▨ Supervisor (Non-Arch)
■ Project Manager

DETAILS

NV BLM Permitable as "Principal Investigator": **Historic**, Statewide; **Prehistoric**: Statewide

MSHA Certification valid until June 31, 2013.

Register of Professional Archaeologists member since May 2011.

Society for American Archaeology member since 2010.

Member of the Nevada Archaeological Association

Member of the Nevada Mining Association

Member of the Geological Society of Nevada

WORK EXPERIENCE DETAIL

Digital Technologies in Archaeological Consulting LLC
- Sparks, Nevada
- January 2013 to Present
- Principal Investigator
- Responsibilities
  - Business Development
  - Report Writing and Project Management
  - Report editing
  - Design and Implementation of digital recording procedures
  - Responsible for all phases of archaeological work

Chambers Group, Inc.
- Reno, Nevada
- January 2012 to November 2012
- Permitted as Principal Investigator statewide for prehistoric and historic resources
- Key Projects
  - *Digital 395 Project*
    - Included the recordation of all types of historic resources along U.S. Highway 395 from Reno, NV to Barstow, CA.
    - Total work time in California for this project was approximately six months. An additional three months was spent on site record digitization and report writing.
- Responsibilities
  - Report Writing and Small Project Management
  - Site recording in Nevada and California
  - Report editing
  - Site record editing and digitization
  - Leading crews for survey and site recording

Kautz Environmental Consultants
- Sparks, Nevada
- June 14, 2011 to October 2011
- Responsibilities
  - Field Technician - 6.14.11 - 8.14.11
    - Historic and prehistoric artifact identification
    - Site recording and survey
  - Crew Chief
    - Manage a four-person crew for survey and site recording
    - Site documentation including IMACS and associated forms
    - Site and artifact photography
    - Feature identification and description
    - Site recording using Magellan MobileMapper and ESRI ArcPad software

Western Cultural Resource Management, Inc
- Sparks, Nevada
- August 10, 2010 to June 6, 2011
- Responsibilities
  - Field Technician - 8.10.10 to 9.6.10
    - Controlled excavation

Chris Webster - 2

- Artifact identification
- Crew Chief - 9.7.10 to June 6, 2011
  - Directed crews of 10-15 technicians during excavation and surveying activities
  - Site mapping using a Total Station and a Trimble GPS unit
  - Soil analysis and identification
  - Artifact identification
  - Detailed field inventory records using IMACS forms
  - Survey and site recording activities

Southeastern Archaeological Services, Inc
- Brunswick, Georgia
- June, 2010
- Sites
  - Phase II shovel testing and unit excavation on an early 18th century slave quarters and two prehistoric, Woodland Period, shell middens

Pacific Legacy
- Northern Nevada
- March 2009 to July 2009
- Crew Chief, as needed, during the season
- Field Technician
- Responsibilities
  - Site Recording using IMACS forms
  - Prehistoric and historic sites across northern Nevada
  - In-field analysis of artifacts
  - Site map drawing, artifact sketching
  - Recorded sites with handheld Trimble GPS units

AMEC, Inc.
- Granite Falls, Washington
- December 8, 2008 to March 2009
- Crew Chief
  - Prehistoric Phase III Excavation on Olcott sites 45SN303 and 45SN28.
  - Lithic analysis and identification
  - Test Unit profiling and mapping
  - Complete site mapping with a Nikon Total Station and data collector using TDS SurveyPro software
  - Munsell color analysis

Pacific Legacy
- Northern Nevada
- September 23, 2008 to November 20, 2008
- Field Technician
  - Site Recording
  - Prehistoric and historic sites across northern Nevada
  - In-field analysis of artifacts
  - Site map drawing and artifact sketching
  - Recorded sites with a handheld Trimble GPS unit
  - Recorded on IMACS forms

Chris Webster - 3

Kautz Environmental Consultants
- Winnemucca, Nevada
- August 26, 2008 to September 18, 2008
- Field Technician
  - Pedestrian Survey
  - Prehistoric and historic, in-field, artifact analysis including lithics, tin cans, and historic glass.
  - Used Thales GPS device for recording and mapping

Montgomery Archaeological Consultants
- Various Locations in Utah
- May 19, 2008 to August 19, 2008
- Field Technician
  - Pedestrian Survey in the Uintah Basin in northeastern Utah
    - 7-10 mile transects in varying weather conditions over desert rock and sand
    - Located prehistoric sites as well as historic sheep-herding sites
    - Seismic pedestrian survey
  - Excavation
    - 1 m x 1 m and 1 m x 2 m test units near Kanab, Utah
    - Prehistoric and historic sites
  - Equipment Used
    - Trimble GeoXH handheld GPS with TerraSync
    - Trimble handheld with external antenna

Southwest Archaeological Consultants
- Northwestern New Mexico
- March 6, 2008 to May 4, 2008
- Field Technician
  - Various prehistoric Phase II excavation units for the El Segundo Mine Project
  - Transit used to take elevations and coordinate units
  - Identification of prehistoric features and artifacts relating to the Southwest

ASC Group, Inc.
- Wilmington, Ohio
- January 21, 2008 to February 28, 2008
- Field Technician
  - Various prehistoric Phase II excavations for the REX East Pipeline
  - Backhoe trenching to search for features
  - 5 m interval, 50 cm x 50 cm shovel testing
  - Worked in sub-zero temperatures and high winds

S&ME, Inc.
- Southeastern United States
- Temporary Field Technician from October 30, 2006 to January 25, 2007
  - 1200 acre Phase I in Wilmington, NC
  - Paleo-archaic to Late Woodland artifacts
- Crew Chief from January 26, 2007 to January 6, 2008
  - Large scale Phase I surveys in South Carolina, North Carolina, and Virginia
  - Large scale Phase II in Wilmington, North Carolina
  - Large scale Phase III in Wilmington, North Carolina with six field technicians under supervision

Chris Webster - 4

- Writing
  - Investigated and wrote reports for three reconnaissance surveys: 1200 acres, 500 acres, and 25 acres

Louis Berger Group
- Burlington and Stowe, Vermont
- September 25, 2006 to October 27, 2006
- Field Technician
  - Phase I surveys for the VELCO project
  - Weather conditions were cold and wet with gear packed in every day

Janus Research, Inc.
- Tampa, Florida
- July 17, 2006 to September 22, 2006
- Field Technician
  - Phase I survey on Everglades Reclamation Project for the South Florida Water Management District

Alpine Archaeology
- Northwestern Colorado
- June 6, 2006 to June 27, 2006
- Field Technician
  - Site Number 5MF5389, Craig, CO
    - Paleo-archaic excavations
    - Phase III excavations

Archaeological Historical Conservancy
- Miami, Florida
- December 13, 2005 to May 15, 2006
- Principle Investigator: C. Ya Later
- Project Director: B. Jones
- Field Technician
  - Project 8DA11
  - Excavated through
    - Royal Palm Hotel, 1897-1930
    - Fort Dallas, 1860s
    - Tequesta Indian burial site, pre-1760s
    - Human remains excavation and identification
    - Water screening
    - Created new procedures and documents for certain elements of the site excavation

Great Lakes Archaeological Research Center
- East Grand Forks, Minnesota
- October 24, 2005 to November 11, 2005
- Principle Investigator: J. Hanney
- Field Technician
  - 5 cm level excavation
  - Water flotation on site
  - Water screening on site
  - Unit profile drawing
  - Artifact identification

Chris Webster - 5

Earthwatch Institute Field School
- Olduvai Gorge, Tanzania
- September 21, 2005 to October 13, 2005
- Principle Investigator: Fidelis T. Masao, Open University of Tanzania
- Training received
  - Excavation techniques
  - Drawing sections of stratigraphy
  - Recognition of artifacts and fossils
  - Identification of skeletal parts and the species the represent
  - Analysis of artifacts and bone
- Lectures received at the site
  - Discovery of Olduvai Gorge and subsequent paleoanthropological research
  - The geology and interpretation of the DK area and west up to the JK site
  - Geology of Olduvai
  - Paleoenvironments and climates
  - Olduvai hominids in geological and associated industries background
  - Landscape archaeology approaches to hominid land use
  - Actualistic studies and the use of modern analogs such as the Serengeti ecosystem, Lake Makat in the Ngorongoro Crater, and Lakes Natron and Manyara
  - Culture, legends and lore of the neighboring Maasai people

---

Chris Webster - 6

MILITARY EDUCATION AND EXPERIENCE

Naval Air Technical Training Center
- Millington, Tennessee
- September 1993 to May 1994
- Certificate of Completion for Avionics Technician Course

Naval Air Technical Training Center
- Millington, Tennessee
- May 1994 to July 1994
- Certificate of Completion for Avionics Systems Integration Course (Advanced Avionics)

Naval Enlisted Aviation Warfare Specialist Training
- August 1995 to December 1997
- Ongoing training in aviation warfare techniques and leadership responsibilities

United States Navy
- June 1993 to December 1997
- Aviation Electronics Technician
- Rank E-5, Petty Officer Second Class, upon discharge
- Responsibilities
  - Shortly after joining Tactical Electronic Warfare Squadron 132 in Whidbey Island, Washington, I completed the training for Line Division Plane Captain. This required me to interact with the pilots in the squadron for starting the aircraft and taxiing and shutdown after the mission. I was also responsible for the daily and turn-around inspections on the aircraft.
  - Within six months I was appointed Night Shift Supervisor. My shift was responsible for all of the scheduled maintenance on the aircraft as well as preparing the aircraft for the next day's mission and preparing briefs for the pilots.
  - As Shift Supervisor, I was in charge of between 8 and 15 men and was required to conduct performance reviews and counseling.
  - As Supervisor, I was also in charge of training for my entire shop. I administered training courses and maintained training folders for approximately 20-25 men.
  - As Training Supervisor I implemented a new organizational system for our shop that was more efficient and more easily understood. The system was soon implemented by the rest of the squadron and then by the rest of the Air Wing.
  - On the U.S.S. Enterprise I worked on the flight deck during night time operations. This required substantial amounts of teamwork and organization. There were constantly planes taking off, landing, or taxiing, or some combination of all three requiring detailed attention to duty and observation of my surroundings.

Chris Webster - 7

C O M P U T E R S   A N D   T E C H N O L O G Y

Proficient with the following software
- Microsoft Office
- Apple iWork
- Surfer 9.0
- Adobe Illustrator and Photoshop
- ESRI ArcGIS Suite
- Open source QGIS

Computer Systems
- Windows Operating System
- Mac OSX
- Apple iOS (iPhone and iPad)
- Android 4.1 and higher

Current Projects
- Book: A Guide for living as a Shovelbum
- Random Acts of Science archaeology blog focusing on education and outreach.
- CRM Archaeology Podcast
- Research and development of an IMACS Site Recording application for use on the versatile iPad platform from Apple, Inc.
- Research and development of a projectile point identification application for Apple iOS devices.
- Research and development of a Nevada Experience application for iOS.

Chris Webster - 8

138

Davy "Bagman" Fieldman, Esq.
Archaeological Field Technician

1492 Columbus Dr.
Miami, FL 99432
prodigger@gmail.com
(775) 555-4545

Summary

An ambitious, teachable archaeological technician with a proven track record of contributing to the success of archaeological work wherever I go.

Archaeology Consulting, LLC

Ran crews of four technicians in archaeology survey and excavation.

Select Accomplishments

- **Capable**: Employed on various cultural resource management projects in Nevada, California, and Utah.
- **Astute**: A team player that quickly grasps the methods, techniques, and recordation systems of different companies.
- **Enthusiastic**: Always takes the initiative to go the extra mile in order to assure each task is accomplished correctly the first time.

Professional Experience

Cultural Resource Specialists

Ran crews of three to four techs for pedestrian survey on active mines.

Crew Chief Archaeology Consulting, LLC, Big Rocks, Utah (2010 – 2013)
Crew Chief Cultural Resource Specialists, Ely, Nevada (2008 – 2010)
Archaeological Technician James Riley Environmental, St. Charles, California (2005 – 2008)
Archaeological Technician Archaeology Professionals, Inc., Vernal, Utah (2002 – 2005)
Laboratory Technician University of Archaeology Laboratory of Archaeology, Four Points, California (2002)

Education

Bachelor of Arts: Archaeology, University of Archaeology, (2002)

Technical Skills

James Riley Environmental

Operated a Trimble GPS and a digital camera during site recording on pedestrian survey.

- Archaeological survey, monitoring, photography and excavation
- Artifact collection, processing, and curation
- Experienced in Microsoft Office programs and Trimble applications
- Proficient with Apple iOS devices and programming
- Valid Nevada driver's license and clean driving record

> *"Davy is one of the most dedicated and motivated techs we have every employed at this company. He will be sorely missed."* James Riley, President, James Riley Environmental, St. Charles, California.

Please contact me right away to learn exactly how I can help your company:
(775) 555-4545
http://www.linkedin.com/pub/davy-fieldman/

APPENDIX B: COVER LETTER EXAMPLES

Cover Letters are discussed in chapter 3. What follows are three examples of the three most common types of cover letters, including: the Invited Cover Letter, the Prospecting Cover Letter, and the Networking Cover Letter.

Invited Cover Letter

Your Address
City, State, Zip Code

Date
Admin (or Human Resources)
Company Applying To
City, State (of company)

Subject: Shovelbums Post

To Whom It May Concern (or name of Human Resources person if known), I saw your posting for summer fieldwork on the Shovelbums.org website on April 30. The posting was for work out of your Lexington, Kentucky office.

Currently, I'm working in southern Indiana on a project similar to the one that was advertised. This project is slated to end on May 12. I have four years of experience on projects similar to the one listed, and, two years in the same region. I'd like to be considered for a field technician position, or if available, a crew chief position.

I've attached my CV and references to this email. You can reach me for questions or concerns at (phone number) and at (chriswebster@digtech-llc.com). Please, feel free to call, or email, me with questions or concerns regarding my CV and my qualifications for this position.

Thank you,
Chris Webster
Enclosures (2)

Prospecting Cover Letter

Your Address
City, State, Zip Code

Date
Admin (or Human Resources)
Company applying to
City, State (of company)

Subject: Upcoming Fieldwork

To Whom It May Concern (or name of Human Resources person if known), I'm an experienced field technician who's worked in this region for the past five years. Three years ago, I worked for your firm on the Really Big PipeLine project (Report number, or site number, if known). The project lasted for three months and included intensive survey that included shovel testing every 30-meters along the pipeline.

Currently, I'm finishing up the winter months by brushing up on a few regional archaeological works and I'm reading some relevant papers. I was wondering if you have a need for experienced field technicians as the field season gets closer?

I've attached my CV and references to this email. Please contact me when you have an upcoming project that will need to be staffed. I can be reached for questions or concerns at (phone number) and at (chrisweb ster@digtech-llc.com).

Thank you,
Chris Webster
Enclosures (2)

Networking Cover Letter

Your Address
City, State, Zip Code

Date
Name of Former Employer
Company
City, State

Subject: Possible Fieldwork

Mr./Ms. (Name of Contact),
I worked with your firm on several projects during the last field season. I've been working several states away for the last few months but now I'm returning to the region.

I'm wondering if your firm has any upcoming projects that I could participate in? Or, do you know of any projects coming up in the area that I could inquire about? I'm willing to work on a variety of project in either a field technician or crew chief capacity.

I've attached my CV and references to this email. Please call me if you have, or know of, any upcoming projects that I could participate in. I can be reached for questions or concerns at (phone number) and at (chriswebster@digtech-llc.com).

Thank you,
Chris Webster
Enclosures (2)

APPENDIX C: FIELDWORK CHECKLIST

I make lists for everything. When I'm getting ready to go on a field project, I refer to my various lists as to what I need to bring. On the sample list below, I've made separate categories that relate to different types of projects. Feel free to use these lists, modify them, or create your own. You don't want to be stuck four hours from the nearest town without your underwear. It's happened.

Every Trip Items - Clothing
- Work pants
- Work shirts
- Work socks
- Casual pants/shorts
- Casual shirts
- Casual socks
- Work boots
- Shoes/sandals
- Underwear
- Belt
- Work hat
- Casual hat
- Swim shorts
- Work jacket
- Work gloves
- Winter gear

Every Trip Items – Food
- Breakfast items
- Lunch items
- Prepared dinners
- Coffee/tea
- Utensils
- Spices
- Plates
- Water heater
- French press
- Rice cooker

- ☐ Hand towels
- ☐ Sponge
- ☐ Dish soap
- ☐ 5 gallon water container
- ☐ Espresso machine (that might just be on my list . . .)
- ☐ Travel mug
- ☐ Water bottles

Survey Items

- ☐ Survey backpack
- ☐ Water reservoir for backpack
- ☐ Hiking boots
- ☐ Field hat
- ☐ Sunscreen
- ☐ Compass
- ☐ GPS
- ☐ Field notebook (or tablet)
- ☐ Pencils
- ☐ Safety Vest
- ☐ Hard Hat
- ☐ Handkerchief
- ☐ Tape measure
- ☐ Clipboard
- ☐ Toilet paper
- ☐ Sun glasses

Testing/Excavation Items

- ☐ Clipboard
- ☐ Dig kit
- ☐ Safety vest
- ☐ Hard hat
- ☐ Field hat
- ☐ Field boots
- ☐ Folding ruler
- ☐ Compass
- ☐ Tape measure
- ☐ Trowels (pointed and square)
- ☐ Hammer
- ☐ Chaining pins
- ☐ Water bottles

- ☐ Spray bottle
- ☐ Toilet paper
- ☐ Sun glasses

Camping

- ☐ Tent
- ☐ Bedding / cot / air mattress
- ☐ Pillows
- ☐ Headlamp
- ☐ Folding chair

Extra Camping Gear

- ☐
- ☐
- ☐
- ☐
- ☐

APPENDIX D: INTERVIEW QUESTIONS

When you are offered a job in CRM archaeology, it's usually by phone. After applying to a number of positions, you'll get a call from a potential employer asking if you are still available and if you can start when they want you too. Many people don't ask questions of the interviewer before taking the job. The perceptive field technician will ask, at a minimum, the questions below.

- How much does the position pay?
- What is the pay range for my position (so you know where your experience got you)?
- How much is the per diem?
- When will I receive my first paycheck after starting? Will it be for a full pay period?
- How often are paychecks distributed?
- Do you use direct deposit?
- How is per diem paid (check or cash)?
- When is per diem paid (beginning of the session/week, with the paycheck, daily, or at the end of the session)?
- How long are the workdays, and what is the work schedule?
- Does drive time to and from the project area count for the workday?
- Will we be camping? If so, what equipment is provided by your company?
- Is there a rain/snow day policy?
- If I need a sick day, am I expected to return my per diem?
- What phase is the project (survey, testing, excavation, etc.)?
- Are we expecting to find more historic or prehistoric sites?
- What are the time periods of the expected sites?
- Do you have any reference material that you could direct me to related to the site types that are expected?
- What sort of terrain is the project area in?
- Can you tell me anything else about the project area that I should know?
- How long is the project expected to last?

- Do you expect to have more work immediately following this project?
- Will this position possibly lead to a full-time position?
- If this is an excavation, are there expected to be any lab positions available following the fieldwork?

These are just some of the questions I've asked in the past. You should ask the questions that are appropriate for the job you're applying for. Don't forget to read the job posting again. You don't want to ask something they already answered.

APPENDIX E: DIMENSIONAL LUMBER

Lumber can be used to date an historic site, especially in the desert west were preservation is high. Below are sample tables indicating the difference between the nominal dimension of wood and the actual measurement after the wood has been milled and dried. Generally, between the mid-1800s and approximately 1920, wood sizes should closely match the nominal dimension. After 1920, the measured size starts to shrink. Table 1 shows the standards that were set in 1964 and are still used today. Remember, though, that lumber on very remote sites was possibly milled on site and could have been milled to any standard of size.[1]

TABLE E1. Lumber sizes as of the 1964 American Lumber Standards.[1]

NOMINAL DIMENSION (in)	STANDARD DRY DIMENSION (in)	EQUIVALENT GREEN DIMENSION (in)
2	$1\frac{2}{3}$	$1\frac{17}{32}$
3	$2\frac{5}{8}$	$2\frac{11}{16}$
4	$3\frac{5}{8}$	$3\frac{11}{16}$
6	$5\frac{1}{2}$	$5\frac{5}{8}$
8	$7\frac{1}{2}$	$7\frac{11}{16}$
10	$9\frac{1}{2}$	$9\frac{3}{4}$
12	$11\frac{1}{2}$	$11\frac{13}{16}$

1 U.S. Forest Products Laboratory *History of Yard Lumber Size Standards.* (U.S. Dept of Agriculture: Madison, WI, 1964).

TABLE E2. SAMPLE LUMBER SIZES, 1914.[2]

NOMINAL DIMENSION (in)	MILLED DIMENSIONS (in)						
	WHITE & NORWAY PINE	NORTH CAROLINA PINE	LONGLEAF PINE	LONGLEAF & SHORTLEAF PINE	DOUGLAS FIR, WESTERN HEMLOCK, CEDAR, & SPRUCE	HEMLOCK & TAMARACK	IDAHO WHITE PINE, WESTERN PINE, FIR & LARCH
2 × 4	$1\frac{5}{8} \times 3\frac{5}{8}$	$1\frac{3}{4} \times 3\frac{3}{4}$	$1\frac{5}{8} \times 3\frac{5}{8}$	$1\frac{5}{8} \times 3\frac{5}{8}$	$1\frac{5}{8} \times 3\frac{5}{8}$	$1\frac{3}{4} \times 3\frac{5}{8}$	$1\frac{5}{8} \times 3\frac{5}{8}$
2 × 6	$1\frac{5}{8} \times 5\frac{5}{8}$	$1\frac{3}{4} \times 5\frac{3}{4}$	$1\frac{5}{8} \times 5\frac{5}{8}$	$1\frac{5}{8} \times 5\frac{5}{8}$	$1\frac{5}{8} \times 5\frac{5}{8}$	$1\frac{3}{4} \times 5\frac{3}{4}$	$1\frac{5}{8} \times 5\frac{1}{2}$
2 × 8	$1\frac{5}{8} \times 7\frac{5}{8}$	$1\frac{3}{4} \times 7\frac{3}{4}$	$1\frac{5}{8} \times 7\frac{5}{8}$	$1\frac{5}{8} \times 7\frac{1}{2}$	$1\frac{5}{8} \times 7\frac{1}{2}$	$1\frac{3}{4} \times 7\frac{3}{4}$	$1\frac{5}{8} \times 7\frac{1}{2}$
2 × 10	$1\frac{5}{8} \times 9\frac{5}{8}$	$1\frac{3}{4} \times 9\frac{3}{4}$	$1\frac{5}{8} \times 9\frac{5}{8}$	$1\frac{5}{8} \times 9\frac{1}{2}$	$1\frac{5}{8} \times 9\frac{1}{2}$	$1\frac{3}{4} \times 9\frac{3}{4}$	$1\frac{5}{8} \times 9\frac{1}{2}$
2 × 12	$1\frac{5}{8} \times 11\frac{5}{8}$	$1\frac{3}{4} \times 11\frac{3}{4}$	$1\frac{5}{8} \times 11\frac{5}{8}$	$1\frac{5}{8} \times 11\frac{1}{2}$	$1\frac{5}{8} \times 11\frac{1}{2}$	$1\frac{3}{4} \times 11\frac{3}{4}$	$1\frac{5}{8} \times 11\frac{1}{2}$

2 Royal S. Kellog, *Lumber and Its Uses* (Scientific Book Corp.: New York, 1914).

APPENDIX F: WINTER CHECKLIST

For an archaeologist, preparation for winter depends on where you live or work. For some, there is no preparation. Work continues, and they work year-round. For others, work stops when the snow falls, and they either have to find something else to do, live off savings, or move to another region where work is continuing. Preparing for the winter takes planning. The following is a list of things you can do to help prepare you for either working, or not working, for the winter. These are just suggestions, and you should do what is right for you.

Early Spring
- Figure out how many months you could potentially be out of work next winter. If this is your first season, plan on three or four months.
- Estimate your bills and living expenses for one month. Multiply your monthly expenses by the number of months you think you'll be out of work. Add 15%. This is your savings goal for the field season. The 15% is to cover you between jobs during the field season.
- You're pay and per diem should be fairly consistent throughout the field season. Divide the amount of money you need to save by the number of paychecks you're likely to receive. This is the amount per paycheck you need to save. Either increase that amount early on and adjust later, or stay consistent throughout the season. I would suggest saving more early on so you can be flexible at the end of the season.

Summer
- Start thinking about what you want to do over the winter: work or relax.
- If you want to work, keep an eye out for long-term projects that could take you up to, or through, the winter. You might have to move to another region for the work.
- Look for major excavations that are advertised near the end of the summer. Often, lab work for those projects will continue through the winter.
- If you want to travel, start making a travel plan. Sketch out your destinations, accommodations, method of travel (buying train passes, etc.), and travel times.

- If you want to relax, start thinking about where you'd like to spend the winter. If it's with friends and family, stay in contact with them so it's not a total surprise when you show up for a few weeks in January.
- Check your savings plan to make sure you're on track with your goals. Adjust as necessary.

Fall Planning

- Planning to work? Contact companies currently on major excavations and ask about possible lab work. Be prepared to work for no per diem.
- Planning to travel? Make sure you have plane tickets, hostel/hotel reservations, passes, and whatever else your trip requires ready to go.
- Planning to stay with friends and family? Make sure you've called, or been in contact with, everyone you plan to stay with. Put it on your calendar if you plan to move around. I'd take this opportunity to see different people in different places. Be a gracious houseguest. Help with cleaning and cooking. Pitch in with the utilities if they are letting you stay there for free.

Winter

- Start thinking about work in the spring.
- Contact companies you worked with during the last field season.
- Contact friends you worked with.
- Update your CV.
- Check your finances and start thinking about your goals for next winter.

INDEX

ABOUT THE AUTHOR

Chris Webster has an MS from the University of Georgia in archaeological resource management and has been doing CRM archaeology since 2005. He's worked as a shovelbum in 17 states and for multiple companies. Chris and his wife traveled around the country working from job to job for several years before he decided to get his Master's degree. Now, as the owner of his own CRM firm, Digital Technologies in Archaeological Consulting, LLC, Chris is striving to bring the world of CRM archaeology to as many people as he can through books, blogging, and podcasting.

Chris has a popular archaeology blog called Random Acts of Science and he hosts a podcast called the CRM Archaeology Podcast. This book is the culmination of the blog's popular "Shovelbums Guide" series in which Chris covers much of what is contained in this book.

As a prolific blogger, podcaster, and now author, Chris plans to continue writing books about the lifestyle associated with CRM archaeology and hopes that more people will be encouraged to stay in this dynamic, challenging, and ultimately rewarding field.